First World War
and Army of Occupation
War Diary
France, Belgium and Germany

25 DIVISION
74 Infantry Brigade,
Brigade Machine Gun Company
10 March 1916 - 28 February 1918

WO95/2247/5

The Naval & Military Press Ltd
www.nmarchive.com
Published in association with The National Archives

Published by

The Naval & Military Press Ltd

Unit 10 Ridgewood Industrial Park,
Uckfield, East Sussex,
TN22 5QE England
Tel: +44 (0) 1825 749494

www.naval-military-press.com
www.nmarchive.com

Contents

Document type	Place/Title	Date From	Date To
Heading	WO95/2247-6		
Heading	74th Machine Gun Coy. Mar 1916 Feb 1918 (Dec 1916 Missing)		
Heading	74th Machine Gun Coy., March, 1916 Dec 16 Missing		
War Diary	Grantham Southampton	10/03/1916	10/03/1916
War Diary	Havre	11/03/1916	14/03/1916
War Diary	Aubigney	15/03/1916	17/03/1916
War Diary	Chelers	17/03/1916	31/03/1916
Heading	74th Machine Gun Coy., April, 1916		
War Diary	Chelers	01/04/1916	11/04/1916
War Diary	Penin	12/04/1916	21/04/1916
War Diary	Camblain	22/04/1916	22/04/1916
War Diary	Trenches	23/04/1916	30/04/1916
Heading	74th Machine Gun Coy., May, 1916		
War Diary		01/05/1916	08/05/1916
War Diary	Trenches	09/05/1916	17/05/1916
War Diary	Camblain	18/05/1916	18/05/1916
War Diary	Villier De Acq	19/05/1916	19/05/1916
War Diary	Bailleul	20/05/1916	31/05/1916
Map	Q Sector (Vimy Ridge)		
Heading	74th Machine Gun Coy., June 1916		
War Diary	Bailleul-Aux-Cornailles	01/06/1916	14/06/1916
War Diary	Framecourt	15/06/1916	15/06/1916
War Diary	St. Acheul	16/06/1916	17/06/1916
War Diary	Fienvillers	18/06/1916	18/06/1916
War Diary	Belettre	19/06/1916	25/06/1916
War Diary	Lavicogne	26/06/1916	27/06/1916
War Diary	Rubempre	28/06/1916	30/06/1916
Heading	74th Machine Gun Company July 1916		
War Diary	Warloy	03/07/1916	03/07/1916
War Diary	Bouzincourt	04/07/1916	04/07/1916
War Diary	Bouzincourt	06/07/1916	06/07/1916
War Diary	Usna Redoubt	06/06/1916	10/06/1916
War Diary	Senlis	10/06/1916	14/06/1916
War Diary	Awbert	14/06/1916	15/06/1916
War Diary	Tara Redoubt	15/06/1916	17/06/1916
War Diary	Forceville	17/06/1916	18/06/1916
War Diary	Beauvam	18/06/1916	21/06/1916
War Diary	Bus-Les Artois	21/06/1916	21/06/1916
War Diary	Bus	24/06/1916	24/06/1916
War Diary	Englebelmer	24/07/1916	24/07/1916
Heading	74th Brigade Machine Gun Company August 1916		
War Diary	Englebelmer	01/08/1916	05/08/1916
War Diary	Beaussart	05/08/1916	07/08/1916
War Diary	Mailly	07/06/1916	07/06/1916
War Diary	Maillet	10/06/1916	10/06/1916
War Diary	Bus-Le-Artois.	10/06/1916	15/06/1916
War Diary	Lealvillers	15/06/1916	17/06/1916
War Diary	Hedauvanne	17/06/1916	19/06/1916
War Diary	Thiepval Wood	19/06/1916	25/06/1916

War Diary	Bouzincourt	19/06/1916	30/06/1916
Heading	74th. M.G. Company M.G.C. September 1916		
War Diary	Ovillers	01/09/1916	06/09/1916
War Diary	Bouzincourt	07/09/1916	07/09/1916
War Diary	Lealvillers	08/09/1916	08/09/1916
War Diary	Puchvillers	10/06/1916	10/06/1916
War Diary	Beauval	11/09/1916	11/09/1916
War Diary	Candas	12/09/1916	12/09/1916
War Diary	Franqueville	13/09/1916	25/09/1916
War Diary	Forceville	26/09/1916	27/09/1916
War Diary	Hedauville	27/09/1916	27/09/1916
War Diary	Thiepval Wood	28/09/1916	30/09/1916
Heading	74th Machine Gun Coy., October, 1916		
War Diary	Thiepval Wood	01/10/1916	02/10/1916
War Diary	Bouzincourt	03/10/1916	05/10/1916
War Diary	Mouquet Farm	09/10/1916	22/10/1916
War Diary	Albert	23/10/1916	23/10/1916
War Diary	Vadencourt	24/10/1916	24/10/1916
War Diary	Beauval	25/10/1916	31/10/1916
Heading	74th Machine Gun Coy., November, 1916		
War Diary	Caestre	01/11/1916	01/11/1916
War Diary	Meteren	02/11/1916	02/11/1916
War Diary	Nieppe	03/11/1916	03/11/1916
War Diary	Ploegsteert	04/11/1916	30/11/1916
War Diary	Ploegsteert Sector	01/01/1917	01/01/1917
War Diary	28 S.W. 4 Sdition 4A Scals 1/10000	09/01/1917	31/01/1917
War Diary	Ploegsteert Sector	02/02/1917	19/02/1917
War Diary	T26 d.4.2 Caestre.	20/02/1917	20/02/1917
War Diary	Renescure	21/02/1917	21/02/1917
War Diary	Etrehem	22/02/1917	11/03/1917
War Diary	Cormette	14/03/1917	20/03/1917
War Diary	Wallon Cappel	21/03/1917	21/03/1917
War Diary	Strazeele	22/03/1917	31/03/1917
War Diary	Armentieres	01/04/1917	06/04/1917
War Diary	Steent-Je	08/04/1917	11/04/1917
War Diary	Bulford Camp	12/04/1917	12/04/1917
War Diary	Wulverghem Sector	15/04/1917	24/04/1917
War Diary	La Creche	27/04/1917	05/05/1917
War Diary	Bulford Camp Wulverghem Sector	09/05/1917	22/05/1917
War Diary	Ravelsberg	25/05/1917	25/05/1917
War Diary	La Recousse	26/05/1917	28/05/1917
War Diary	La Creche	29/05/1917	04/06/1917
War Diary	Breemeerschen	05/06/1917	05/06/1917
War Diary	Wulverghem Sector	06/06/1917	09/06/1917
War Diary	Dranoutre	11/06/1917	12/06/1917
War Diary	Messines Ridge	13/06/1917	15/06/1917
War Diary	Dranoutre	16/06/1917	16/06/1917
War Diary	Messines Ridge	17/06/1917	23/06/1917
War Diary	Caudescure		
War Diary	Ham-En-Artois	24/06/1917	24/06/1917
War Diary	Estree Blanche	25/06/1917	25/06/1917
War Diary	Hezecques	26/06/1917	21/07/1917
War Diary	Wallon Cappel	24/07/1917	24/07/1917
War Diary	Hondeghem	25/07/1917	25/07/1917
War Diary	Eecke	26/07/1917	26/07/1917
War Diary	Godewaers Velde	27/07/1917	27/07/1917

War Diary	Godevaersvelde K 35 C 05 sh/27	28/07/1917	30/07/1917
War Diary	Sheet 28/1/20000 Gd31	31/07/1917	31/07/1917
War Diary	Dominion Camp Sheet 28 1/20000 GMd 31	01/08/1917	01/08/1917
War Diary	I.12.b.3.7.	02/08/1917	02/08/1917
War Diary	H.21.b. 23	03/08/1917	03/08/1917
War Diary	I 19.C.3.7	04/08/1917	04/08/1917
War Diary	Swan Chateau I.19.C.37	04/08/1917	04/08/1917
War Diary	H.21.b.8.4	06/08/1917	13/08/1917
War Diary	H21Z84	14/08/1917	19/08/1917
War Diary	Sheet 27 (1/40000) J24a 2015	20/08/1917	31/08/1917
War Diary	G24 Central Sheet 28NW	01/09/1917	01/09/1917
War Diary	J1d3.6.w J8c.4.0	02/09/1917	02/09/1917
War Diary	J.7.a.5.5.	05/09/1917	07/09/1917
War Diary	G.23.b	08/09/1917	19/09/1917
War Diary	Auchel	20/09/1917	30/09/1917
Miscellaneous			
War Diary	Auchel	01/10/1917	03/10/1917
War Diary	Oblinghem	04/10/1917	04/10/1917
War Diary	Cambrin Sector	05/10/1917	05/10/1917
War Diary	Annequin Sheet 36B. F23d. 95.95		
War Diary	Cambrin Sector	06/10/1917	01/11/1917
War Diary	Beuvry F14.a.40.20 Sheet 30 t	02/11/1917	06/11/1917
War Diary	Beuvry	07/11/1917	10/11/1917
War Diary	Cambrin Sector	11/11/1917	30/11/1917
War Diary	Cambrin	01/12/1917	01/12/1917
War Diary	Becerry	02/12/1917	02/12/1917
War Diary	Labeuvriere	03/12/1917	04/12/1917
War Diary	Achiet Le-Petit	05/12/1917	05/12/1917
War Diary	Beugnatre	06/12/1917	07/12/1917
War Diary	Beugnatre (Could)	07/12/1917	07/12/1917
War Diary	Moeuvres 1/20,000 C.24. D.19.25726	08/12/1917	20/12/1917
War Diary	Moeuvres 1/20000 C2t D19. 25.26	21/12/1917	23/12/1917
War Diary	Sheet 57c 1/40,000 H10a 90.40	24/12/1917	31/12/1917
Miscellaneous	Relief Orders No 118	29/12/1917	29/12/1917
War Diary	Moeuvres 1/20,000 Pronville Sector	01/01/1918	04/01/1918
War Diary	Sheet 57.c 1/40,000 H. 10 A. 90 H0	05/01/1918	09/01/1918
War Diary	Sheet 57 c H.10 a. 90.40 Camp 28	10/01/1918	12/01/1918
War Diary	Moeuvres 1/20,000 Pronville Sector.	13/01/1918	31/01/1918
Miscellaneous	Relief Orders		
Miscellaneous	Relief Orders No 127		
Miscellaneous	Relief Orders No 128	28/01/1918	28/01/1918
War Diary	Comp 6 (Cold No 28) Sheet 57c H 10.c.8.8.	01/02/1918	02/02/1918
War Diary	C.16.17+23.	03/02/1918	10/02/1918
War Diary	H 10 C.2.5	11/02/1918	12/02/1918
War Diary	G.14.b. 60.75.	13/02/1918	28/02/1918
Miscellaneous	Relief Orders No. 136	09/02/1918	09/02/1918
Miscellaneous	Move Orders No 138	11/02/1918	11/02/1918

25TH DIVISION
74TH INFY BDE

74TH MACHINE GUN COY.
MAR 1916 - FEB 1918
(DEC 1916 MISSING)

74th Inf. Bde.

25th Division

74th MACHINE GUN COY.,

MARCH, 1916.

/

Feb 1918

(Dec 16 missing)

Company disembarked Harve 11.3.16.

from U.K.

Original

Sheet I

Vol I

XXV

Instructions regarding War Diaries and Intelligence Summaries are contained in F. S. Regs., Part II. and the Staff Manual respectively. Title pages will be prepared in manuscript.

WAR DIARY
or
INTELLIGENCE SUMMARY.
(Erase heading not required.)

Army Form C. 2118.

74 M.G. COMPANY MACHINE GUN CORPS No. MARCH 1916 Date —

Place	Date	Hour	Summary of Events and Information	Remarks and references to Appendices
	March			
GRANTHAM	10th	2AM	Entrained at Military station for B.E. Force.	
SOUTHAMPTON		11AM.	Detrained at Docks station. Split up into two parties. 1st party consisting of 6 officers & 45 men to proceed by MONAS QUEEN. 2nd party 3 officers 96 other ranks & all the Transport to sail by HUNTSCRAFF.	
		4PM	Both parties embarked	
		9 PM	Both parties sailed.	WJPL?
HAVRE	11th	8AM	1st party arrived HAVRE, disembarked and marched to Rest Camp No 1.	
		12 Noon	2nd party arrived HAVRE, disembarked and marched to Rest Camp No 1	WJPL?
	14th	6 pm	Entrained at Point 3 Station HAVRE	
	~~15th~~	9.20pm	Left HAVRE	WJPL?
AUBIGNEY	15th	4.30pm	Arrived AUBIGNEY and detrained	
		7 PM	Left AUBIGNEY by route march to BAILLEUL AUX-CORNAILLES.	
		12MN	Arrived ——— do ———	WJPL?
	17th	9AM.	Left BAILLEUL	
CHELERS		10AM	Arrived CHELERS.	WJPL?
	25th	3PM	No1 Section proceeded to the trenches (ETRUN) for 48 hours instruction with 154th Brigade	WJPL?

Sheet 2

Army Form C. 2118.

Instructions regarding War Diaries and Intelligence Summaries are contained in F. S. Regs., Part II. and the Staff Manual respectively. Title pages will be prepared in manuscript.

WAR DIARY
or
INTELLIGENCE SUMMARY.
(Erase heading not required.)

74 M.G. COMPANY No. MARCH Date 1916 MACHINE GUN CORPS

Place	Date	Hour	Summary of Events and Information	Remarks and references to Appendices
	March			
	27th	11AM	No 2 Section proceeded to the trenches for 48 hours instruction with 154th Brigade.	WJPLt
	28th	3PM	No 1 Section returned from trenches.	WJPLt
	29th	11AM	No 3 Section proceeded to the trenches MORDEUIL for 48 hours instruction with 153rd Brigade	WJPLt
	30th	3PM	No 2 Section returned from trenches.	WJPLt
	31st	9AM	~~Company~~ 1 + 2 Sections ~~[illegible]~~ Brigade Field day.	
		10AM	No 4 Section proceeded to the trenches for 48 hours instruction with the 154th Brigade	WJPLt

W J Brattinton Lt for Capt.
Commanding 74th M. G. Company,
Machine Gun Corps.

T2134. Wt. W708–776. 500000. 4/15. Sir J. C. & S.

74th Inf. Bde.

25th Division

74th MACHINE GUN COY.,

APRIL, 1916.

Sheet 3

Instructions regarding War Diaries and Intelligence Summaries are contained in F. S. Regs., Part II. and the Staff Manual respectively. Title pages will be prepared in manuscript.

WAR DIARY
or
INTELLIGENCE SUMMARY.
(Erase heading not required.)

Army Form C. 2118.

74 M.G. COMPANY No. APRIL Date 1916 MACHINE GUN CORPS

Place	Date	Hour	Summary of Events and Information	Remarks and references to Appendices
	April			
CHELERS	1st	4PM	No 3 Section returned from the trenches.	WJPL
	3rd	5PM	No 4 Section returned from the trenches.	WJPL
	4th to 10th		Company Training	WJPL
	11th	10.30 AM	Left CHELERS for PENIN.	WJPL
		11.30 AM	Arrived PENIN.	WJPL
PENIN	12th to 20th		Company Training.	WJPL
	21st	12.30PM	The Transport proceeded to MONT. ST ELOY with Guns & Equipment.	
		3PM	Nos 1.2.&3 Sections proceeded to MONT. ST ELOY	
		7PM	Nos 1.2.3 Sections with Guns & Equipment proceeded to the trenches & took over from 138th M.G.Coy	
		8PM	Transport moved into Billets at Camblain ABBE.	WJPL
CAMBLAIN	22nd	9AM	No 4 Section moved from PENIN to CAMBLAIN ABBE	WJPL
TRENCHES	23rd		Except for occasional shelling the two	WJPL MAP No 1
	24th		days passed over very quiet	WJPL
	25th		A Mine was blown up in front of our Line about 2 AM.	WJPL
	26th	3.30AM	Heavy Bombardment by the enemy, exploded a mine & rushed the crater.	WJPL

T2134. Wt. W708-776. 500000. 4/15. Sir J. C. & S.

Sheet 4

Instructions regarding War Diaries and Intelligence Summaries are contained in F. S. Regs., Part II. and the Staff Manual respectively. Title pages will be prepared in manuscript.

WAR DIARY
or
INTELLIGENCE SUMMARY.
(Erase heading not required.)

Army Form C. 2118.

74 M. G. COMPANY No. APRIL Date 1916 MACHINE GUN CORPS

Place	Date	Hour	Summary of Events and Information	Remarks and references to Appendices
	April			
Trenches	26th	3.30pm	Two guns from Nos 2 + 3 Sections opened fire on small groups of the Enemy going up to the craters putting about 20 men out of action. Fire was opened on a bombing party of about 15 to 20 men on the lip of the craters putting them all out of action. Lt GILLIES was severely wounded	WJBL
	27th		No action took place of any importance. 1 OR wounded	WJBL
	28th	2pm	The Enemy exploded a mine on our Right Flank. Two of our guns were trained on the craters covering our working parties	WJBL
	29th	6pm	Nos 1 + 2 Section in the Support trench was relieved by Nos 3 + 4 Sections. No 2 Section returned to Billets for 7 days rest. No 1 Section taking over Reserve.	WJBL
	30th	6.50pm	A mine was exploded by the Enemy, + occupied by them. The Enemy's Artillery was very Active during the night, but no damage done.	WJBL

W J Brattenton Lt for Capt.
Commanding 74th M. G. Company,
Machine Gun Corps.

T2134. Wt. W708–776. 500000. 4/15. Sir J. C. & S.

74th Inf. Bde.

25th Division

74th MACHINE GUN COY.,

MAY, 1916.

Sheet 5

Instructions regarding War Diaries and Intelligence Summaries are contained in F. S. Regs., Part II. and the Staff Manual respectively. Title pages will be prepared in manuscript.

WAR DIARY
or
INTELLIGENCE SUMMARY.
(Erase heading not required.)

Army Form C. 2118.

74 M.G. COMPANY MACHINE GUN No. MAY 1916 Date

Place	Date	Hour	Summary of Events and Information	Remarks and references to Appendices
	MAY			
	1st	6.50 PM	Left of Q Sector Enemy exploded a mine. Enemy Artillery put a heavy Barrage over ZOUAVE VALLEY & bombarded supports with trench Mortars, little damage was done.	WJPL
	2nd	10 PM	The Enemy exploded a mine in Q89 & occupied the crater.	WJPL
	3rd		our Artillery was very active on the left of Q sector, their fire appeared to be very effective	WJPL
	4th		Quiet day.	WJPL
	5th	1-15AM	Enemy bombed our forward Bombing post at Q90. Attack was not strong, we replied with our Machine Guns. A shock of an explosion was felt at 4-15 AM probably a camouflet opposite Q91.	WJPL
	5th	7.42 PM	Enemy attacked Q89 & 90 the attack was beaten off, our Machine Gun fire appeared to be very effective	WJPL
	6th	12 Noon	No 1 & 2 Sections relieved No 3 & 4 Sections in the Support Trench, No 3 Section Section returned to Rest Billets No 4 Section took over Reserve. Artillery (Enemy) was very active during the day, but no damage done.	WJPL
	7th		A quiet day in Q Sector.	WJPL
	8th	7.50 PM	Enemy exploded a mine opposite Q90. We occupied the near lip & consolidated it, our Machine Guns opened fire within a few seconds of the explosion	WJPL

T2134. Wt. W708-776. 500000. 4/15. Sir J. C. & S.

Instructions regarding War Diaries and Intelligence Summaries are contained in F. S. Regs., Part II. and the Staff Manual respectively. Title pages will be prepared in manuscript.

WAR DIARY
or
INTELLIGENCE SUMMARY.
(Erase heading not required.)

Army Form C. 2118.

74 M.G. COMPANY MACHINE GUN CORPS No. Sheet 6 Date MAY 1916

Place	Date	Hour	Summary of Events and Information	Remarks and references to Appendices
	May			
TRENCHES	9th		A quiet day & night	WJBL.
	10th	~~[illegible]~~	Generally quiet during the day	
		Night	Our Machine Guns opened Indirect fire at intervals on the enemy craters in Q Sector	WJBL.
	11th		Q Sector was shelled throughout the day. Our Artillery replied.	WJBL.
	12th		The Enemy was very active with rifle grenades during the afternoon. Our Machine Guns replied & done considerable damage.	WJBL.
	13th	12 Nn	Nos 1 & 2 Sections was relieved by Nos 3 & 4 Sections. No 1 Section returned to Rest Billets & No 2 Section took over Reserve.	WJBL.
		7.50pm	Enemy sprung a mine in front of Q 87 the near lip was occupied by us. heavy Artillery Bombardment followed, our Machine Guns were very active during the night.	WJBL.
	14th		Enemy used ~~[illegible]~~ many Trench Mortars throughout the day, our Machine Guns done considerable damage in Q 89.	WJBL. WJBL.
	15th		During the morning everything very quiet	
		9.30pm	We sprung 5 mines along our front from Q 89 – Q 91 and occupied	WJBL.

T2134. Wt. W708–776. 500000. 4/15. Sir J. C. & S.

Sheet 7

Instructions regarding War Diaries and Intelligence Summaries are contained in F. S. Regs., Part II. and the Staff Manual respectively. Title pages will be prepared in manuscript.

WAR DIARY
or
INTELLIGENCE SUMMARY.
(Erase heading not required.)

Army Form C. 2118.

Place	Date	Hour	Summary of Events and Information	Remarks and references to Appendices
	May			
TRENCHES	15th		Continued	
			and occupied the rear lip of all the craters.	WJPL
		7-30pm	A heavy Artillery duel lasted from 7-30pm to 9pm 30pm	WJPL
		10pm	One officer & 4 men took a gun up to Z Crater Q90 to consolidate position this gun fired short bursts of fire at Enemys working parties during the night & done considerable damage	WJPL
	16th	12Noon	Enemy Trench mortared support line for about 6 hours.	WJPL
	17th	11AM	Enemy attacked our post on Crater Q88.	WJPL
			The Enemy put on a heavy barrage which prevented reinforcements reaching the crater.	WJPL
		9PM	A counter attack was made, after Artillery preparation, but the enemy were found in Great strength & the counter attack was not successful	WJPL
	18th	4AM	~~The Company~~ 3 & 4 Section was relieved from the trenches by the 140th Coy M.G. Corps	WJPL
CAMBLAIN		2pm	Nos 1, 3 & 4 Sections & Transport moved from CAMBLAIN. ABBE to VILLER DE ACQ	
		10PM	No 2 Section & Headquarters moved from the trenches to VILLER DE. ACQ	WJPL

T2134. Wt. W708-776. 500000. 4/15. Sir J. C. & S.

Sheet 8

Instructions regarding War Diaries and Intelligence Summaries are contained in F. S. Regs., Part II. and the Staff Manual respectively. Title pages will be prepared in manuscript.

WAR DIARY
or
INTELLIGENCE SUMMARY.
(Erase heading not required.)

Army Form C. 2118.

74 M.G. COMPANY No. MAY Date 1916 MACHINE GUN CORPS

Place	Date	Hour	Summary of Events and Information	Remarks and references to Appendices
VILLIER DE ACQ	May 19th	8.30pm	The Company moved from VILLIER DE ACQ to Divisional Area Billets at BAILLEUL AUX CORNAILLES.	WJBLt. WJBLt.
BAILLEUL	20th to 31st		Company & Brigade Training	WJBLt.

W J Brattenton Lt. Capt.
Commanding 74th M.G. Company,
Machine Gun Corps.

T2134. Wt. W708-776. 500000. 4/15. Sir J. C. & S.

"Q" SECTOR (VIMY RIDGE)

74th M. G. COMPANY MACHINE GUN CORPS.

74 M.G. COMPANY
No. ________
Date 5.6.16
MACHINE GUN CORPS

MAP No 1

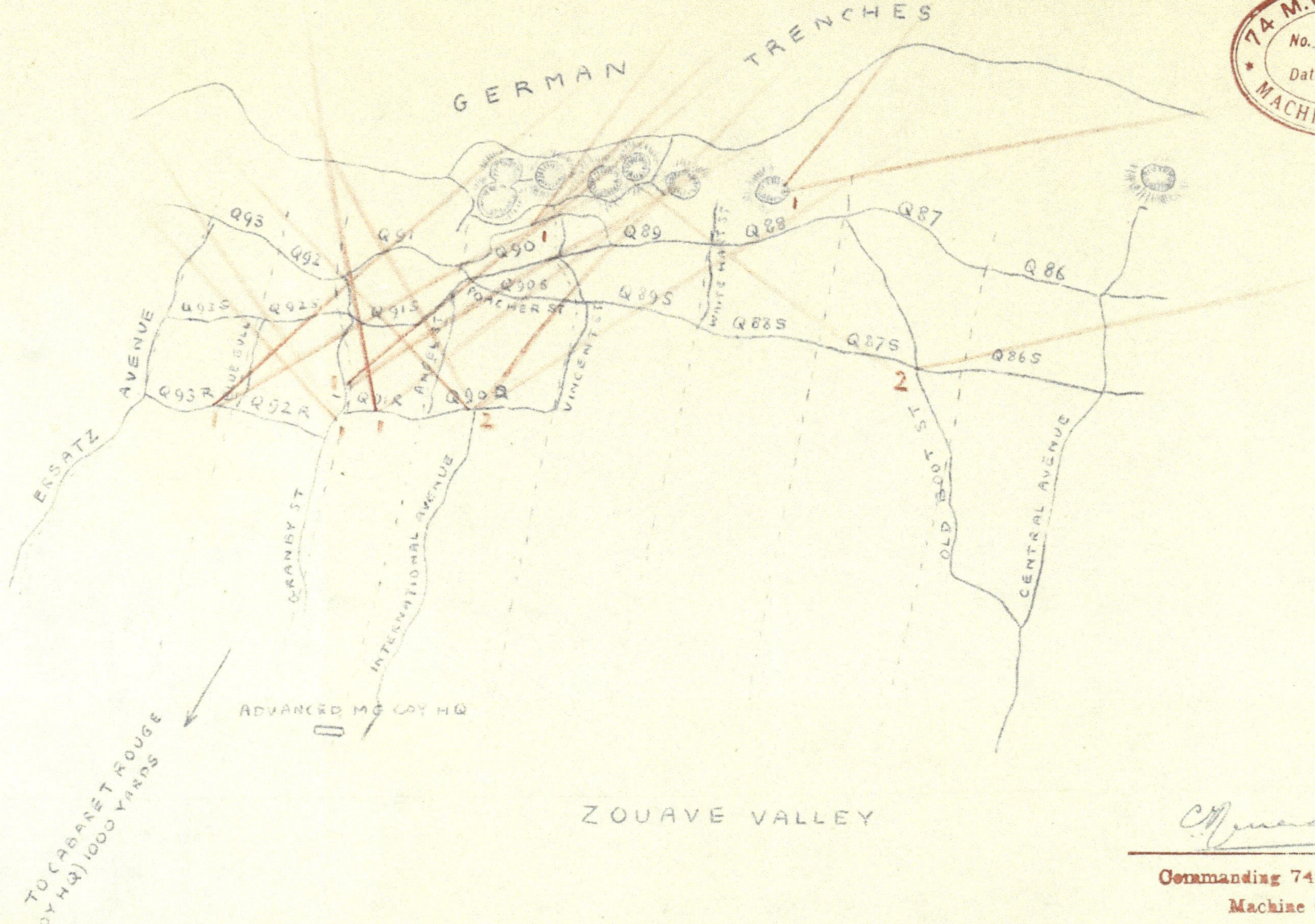

Capt.

Commanding 74th M. G. Company,

Machine Gun Corps.

74th Inf. Bde.

25th Division.

74th MACHINE GUN COY.,

JUNE, 1916.

Instructions regarding War Diaries and Intelligence Summaries are contained in F. S. Regs., Part II. and the Staff Manual respectively. Title pages will be prepared in manuscript.

WAR DIARY
or
INTELLIGENCE SUMMARY.
(Erase heading not required.)

XXV

74 M G Coy

Army Form C. 2118.

Vol 2

Place	Date	Hour	Summary of Events and Information	Remarks and references to Appendices
	JUNE			
BAILLEUL-	1		Company training in conjunction with 9th L.N. LANCASHIRE REGT.	
AUX-CORNAILLES	2		Company Route March & Machine Gun Firing on the Range. ~~[illegible]~~	
"	3		Machine Gun firing on the Range.	
"	4		Staff ride over training area. Advanced Machine Gun drill.	
"	5		Firing on the Range.	
"	6		Company Route March.	
"	7	10AM	G.O.C. 25th Division inspected the Brigade	
"	"	5pm	Brigade night operation in training area.	
"	8		Digging M.G. Emplacements. Stoppages and Immediate Action on the Range	
"	9		Practice in consolidation of trenches and firing on the Range.	
"	10		Digging M.G. Emplacements. Brigade exercise.	
"	11		Digging M.G. Emplacements. Firing on the Range.	
"	12		Brigade exercise. The G.O.C. 25th Division congratulates the Company	
"			on their clean & smart turn out at his recent inspection, particularly	
"			the Transport.	
"	13		Divisional exercise.	

Instructions regarding War Diaries and Intelligence Summaries are contained in F. S. Regs., Part II. and the Staff Manual respectively. Title pages will be prepared in manuscript.

WAR DIARY
or
INTELLIGENCE SUMMARY.
(Erase heading not required.)

Army Form C. 2118.

Place	Date	Hour	Summary of Events and Information	Remarks and references to Appendices
	JUNE			Ref. Map LENS 1/100,000
BAILLEUL AUX-CORNAILLES	14th	10.5 AM	The Company left for FRAMECOURT. Route LIGNY ST. FLOCHEL – TERNAS BUNEVILLE – PT HOUVIN. Arrived FRAMECOURT 3 p.m.	
FRAMECOURT	15th	8.30 AM	The Company marched to ST. ACHEUL. Route:- NUNCQ – LIGNY SUR CANCHE VACQUERIE-LE-BOUCQ – FORTEL – NOEUX – WAVANS – BEAUVOIR-RIVIERE. Arrived at 3.15 p.m.	
ST. ACHEUL	16th		Company training.	
do.	17th	9.45 p.m	The Company marched to FIENVILLERS. Route:- HEUZECOURT – MT. RENAULT FM., – BERNAVILLE. Arrived 1.45 AM. 18th June, 1916.	
FIENVILLERS	18th	9.45 p.m.	The Company marched to BELETTRE FM., BERTEAUCOURT. Route:- BERNEUIL – B. DE. DOMART – DOMART-EN-PONTHIEU – ST. LEGER. Arrived 2.45 A.M. 19th June, 1916	
BELETTRE	19		Practice in concealment of M Guns. Training.	
"	20-24		Company ~~training~~	
	25		G.O.C. 25th Division present at a small tactical scheme carried out by the Company	

Army Form C. 2118.

Instructions regarding War Diaries and Intelligence Summaries are contained in F. S. Regs., Part II. and the Staff Manual respectively. Title pages will be prepared in manuscript.

WAR DIARY
or
INTELLIGENCE SUMMARY.
(Erase heading not required.)

Place	Date	Hour	Summary of Events and Information	Remarks and references to Appendices
	JUNE			Ref. map. LENS $\frac{1}{100,000}$
BEWETTRE	25th	11.8 p.m.	The Company marched to LAVICOGNE. Route:- HALLOY-les-PERNOIS-HAVERNAS-WARGNIES-NAOURS. Arrived 3.45 A.M. 26th June, 1916	
LAVICOGNE	26th		Company training.	
"	27th	10.15 p.m.	The Company marched to RUBEMPRE. Route:- TALMAS-SEPTENVILLE Arrived 1.30 AM. 28th June, 1916.	
RUBEMPRE	28th 29th		Company training	
"	30th		The Company marched to WARLOYBAILLON. Route HERRISART-CONTAY. Arrived 12.50 A.M.	

74th Bde.

25th Div.

WAR
DIARY

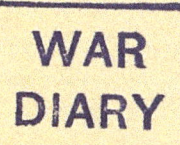

74th MACHINE GUN COMPANY:JULY 1916.

Instructions regarding War Diaries and Intelligence Summaries are contained in F. S. Regs., Part II. and the Staff Manual respectively. Title pages will be prepared in manuscript.

1

WAR DIARY
or
INTELLIGENCE SUMMARY.
(Erase heading not required.)

74 Bde M.G. Coy

Army Form C. 2118.

July

25

Vol 3

Place	Date	Hour	Summary of Events and Information	Remarks and references to Appendices
	July			
WARLOY	3rd	9 pm	Company marched off	
BOUZINCOURT	4th	1.30 am	Arrived.	

Army Form C. 2118.

Instructions regarding War Diaries and Intelligence Summaries are contained in F. S. Regs., Part II. and the Staff Manual respectively. Title pages will be prepared in manuscript.

WAR DIARY
or
INTELLIGENCE SUMMARY.
(Erase heading not required.)

Place	Date	Hour	Summary of Events and Information	Remarks and references to Appendices
	July			Ref. map
BOUZINCOURT	6th	9.30AM.	Left BOUZINCOURT.	57.D.S.E.
USNA REDOUBT	6th	12.1pm.	Arrived USNA REDOUBT. Took over LA BOISELLE from 57 Coy. M.G.C. holding line X.14.C.2.8, X.14.C.7.8, X.14.C.9.5 X.14.d.3.5. Nos. 1 & 2 Sections in LA BOISELLE, No. 3 Sec. ST. ANDREW'S AVE. No 4 Sec. USNA REDOUBT. Company H.Q. at USNA REDOUBT.	1/20,000
do.	7th		Operations enabled 74th Bde. to occupy line X.14.a.9.5, X.14 b.5.2; X.14 d.7.9.	
			No. 2 Section held this line with 4 guns; No. 1 held original line, Nos. 3 & 4 as before. In the course of the fighting No. 2 Section captured a German Machine Gun in action	
do.	8th		We attacked and reoccupied line X.9.C.3.5, X.9.C.7.3 No. 2 Sec. sent 4 guns to this line; No. 1 moved 4 guns up to line previously held by No. 2. No. 4 Sec. sent two guns to LA BOISSELLE. No. 3 Sec. salved 3 Vickers guns	

Instructions regarding War Diaries and Intelligence Summaries are contained in F. S. Regs., Part II. and the Staff Manual respectively. Title pages will be prepared in manuscript.

WAR DIARY
or
INTELLIGENCE SUMMARY.
(*Erase heading not required.*)

Army Form C. 2118.

Place	Date	Hour	Summary of Events and Information	Remarks and references to Appendices
USNA REDOUBT	8th		and two Tripods from MASH VALLEY dropped in the original advance on LA BOISSELLE	
"	9th		Attacked & occupied German Trenches in X. 9. d. Twice counter attacked in the afternoon, we retired on our original line which was our final objective.	
"	10th		Relieved by 7th Co. M.G. Corps. Marched to SENLIS. Total casualties during operations 8 wounded, 3 missing	
SENLIS	10th	8.30pm	Arrived	
	10th 14th		Refitting & overhauling Company	
"	14th	8.30AM	Company marched off	
ALBERT	"	2.30pm	Arrived. Bivouacked for night in field	
"	15	3pm	Left for trenches	
TARA Redoubt	15	6pm	Took over line from 7th MG Coy. Guns distributed as under No 2 Section in trench from X 9 b 4 9 — X 9 b 6 4 with one subsection of No 3. No 1 Section in LA BOISELLE. One subsection No 3 at X 9 d 0 8	

Instructions regarding War Diaries and Intelligence Summaries are contained in F. S. Regs., Part II. and the Staff Manual respectively. Title pages will be prepared in manuscript.

WAR DIARY
or
INTELLIGENCE SUMMARY.
(Erase heading not required.)

Army Form C. 2118.

Place	Date	Hour	Summary of Events and Information	Remarks and references to Appendices
Tara Redoubt	15th		No. 2 Section in Reserve	
	16th	12.30	5th WARWICKS attacked at 2.30 AM from X 3 d 3 0 – X 3 d 0 4	
			and took objective NE of OVILLERS in X 8 b	
	16	8.30 AM	No. 4 Section left gun fired on parties of enemy in the Open	
			between X 2 d 9 4 & X 3 b 0 8. Estimated casualties of enemy 100	
			No 3 Section brought enfilade fire to bear on trenches approaching	
			OVILLERS from E. & NE. After repeated attacks the OVILLERS	
			Garrison surrendered about 6.30 p m	
	17th		Relieved by 143 M G Coy. Total casualties 9 wounded	
FORCEVILLE	17th	9.30 pm	Arrived. via BOUZINCOURT & HEDAUVILLE	
"	18	10.35 AM	Left for BEAUVAL	
BEAUVAL	18	4.35 pm	Arrived via ACHEUX, LEALVILLERS, BEAUQUESNE	
	19th 20th		Cleaning up equipment and Coy training	
	21st	9.30	Left for BUS-LES-ARTOIS	
BUS-LES ARTOIS	21st	6 pm	Arrived. Route: HULEUX, TERRAMESNIL – SARTON – Road Junction just south of THIEVRES – AUTRIE	

T2134. Wt. W708–776. 500000. 4/15. Sir J. C. & S.

5

Army Form C. 2118.

Instructions regarding War Diaries and Intelligence Summaries are contained in F. S. Regs., Part II. and the Staff Manual respectively. Title pages will be prepared in manuscript.

WAR DIARY
or
INTELLIGENCE SUMMARY.
(Erase heading not required.)

Place	Date	Hour	Summary of Events and Information	Remarks and references to Appendices
	JULY			
BUS	24th	8 AM	Left for the line. Relieved 87 M G Coy holding line from Q10c99 to Q17a44. Company H.Q in ENGLEBELMER	
ENGLEBELMER	24th–31st		In the line	

W. Napier Lieut
7th Coy M.G Corps

T2134. Wt. W708-776. 500000. 4/15. Sir J. C. & S.

74th Brigade.
25th Divison

74th BRIGADE.

MACHINE GUN COMPANY

AUGUST 1 9 1 6

Instructions regarding War Diaries and Intelligence Summaries are contained in F. S. Regs., Part II. and the Staff Manual respectively. Title pages will be prepared in manuscript.

WAR DIARY
or
INTELLIGENCE SUMMARY.
(Erase heading not required.)

Army Form C. 2118.

Vol 4

Place	Date	Hour	Summary of Events and Information	Remarks and references to Appendices
			74th M.G. COMPANY MACHINE GUN CORPS.	
ENGLEBELMER	Aug. 1 to Aug. 5		In the line. No operations. 2/Lts N.V. GALLWAY & B.W.T. TYSON (wounded, 1 O.R. wounded	
BEAUSSART	5th		~~Marched~~ Relieved in the line, arrived 11.30 p.m.	
"	7th		Left 6.30 AM for the line. Coy. H.Q at MAILLY MAILLET	
MAILLY MAILLET	7 to 10th		In the line. No operations. No casualties	
"	10th		Relieved in the line.	
BUS-LES-ARTOIS	10th to 14th	2.30 pm	Arrived. via BEAUSSART, BERTRANCOURT Company training.	
"	15th	10.35 AM	Marched off	
LEALVILLERS	15th	1.30 AM	Arrived. via ACHEUX	
"	16th 17th		Company Training	
"	17th		Marched off 3.30 p.m	
HEDAUVILLE	17th	7.30	Arrived via CLAIRFAYE, VARENNES.	

T2131. Wt. W708–776. 500000. 4/15. Sir J. C. & S.

Instructions regarding War Diaries and Intelligence Summaries are contained in F. S. Regs., Part II. and the Staff Manual respectively. Title pages will be prepared in manuscript.

WAR DIARY
or
INTELLIGENCE SUMMARY.
(Erase heading not required.)

Army Form C. 2118.

74th M.G. COMPANY MACHINE GUN CORPS.

Place	Date	Hour	Summary of Events and Information	Remarks and references to Appendices
HEDAUVILLE	18th		O.C. Coy. reconnoitred AUTHUILLE - THIEPVAL	
"	18th	8AM	No. 4 Section proceeded to HAMEL to relieve one Section of 146 Coy in the line	
"	19th	5AM	Remainder of Company proceeded to THIEPVAL WOOD where they took over from 147 MG Coy. Coy. HQ in Wood.	
THIEPVAL WOOD	19th to 25th		In the line. Enemy Artillery appeared to think that an [illegible] was being prepared from this line and frequently put barrages on to our Support and Communication Trenches. On the afternoon of the 25th he opened a heavy bombardment and knocked out two gun teams that were close together in GEMMEL ST. Casualties 4 killed, 5 wounded	
"	25th		Relieved by 146 Coy. Relief carried out with difficulty owing to heavy enemy bombardment.	
BOUZINCOURT	26th	1.40AM	Arrived via AVELUY village	Sheet 57D 1/40,000
	27th to 31st	5AM	Proceeded to line. Took over from 143 & 145 MG Coys in R.32 Anzacs on our right. In the line. No operations	

[illegible] 74 MG Coy.

74th. INFANTRY BDE.

25th. DIVISION

74th. M. G. COMPANY, M. G.C.

S E P T E M B E R 1 9 1 6.

Instructions regarding War Diaries and Intelligence Summaries are contained in F. S. Regs., Part II. and the Staff Manual respectively. Title Pages will be prepared in manuscript.

VOLUME I.

SHEET I.

WAR DIARY
or
INTELLIGENCE SUMMARY
(Erase heading not required.)

Army Form C. 2118.

74th M. G. COMPANY MACHINE GUN CORPS.

Vol 5

Place	Date	Hour	Summary of Events and Information	Remarks and references to Appendices
OVILLERS	1916 Sep 1 to Sep 5		The Company held positions in trenches between LEIPZIG SALIENT & MOUQUET FARM. Casualties 3 OR	
	Sep 6		Relieved by 33 Coy M.G.C. & proceeded to BOUZINCOURT.	
BOUZINCOURT	7		Left BOUZINCOURT & marched to LEALVILLERS	
LEALVILLERS	8		Left LEALVILLERS & marched to PUCHVILLERS	
PUCHVILLERS	10		Left PUCHVILLERS do ~~[illegible]~~ BEAUVAL.	
BEAUVAL	11		" BEAUVAL do CANDAS.	
CANDAS	12		" CANDAS do FRANQUEVILLE.	
FRANQUEVILLE	13		Training & Refitting.	
	14		do. LIEUT. W. J PRATTINTON left the Coy to assume command of the 113 M.G. Coy. 2/Lt. D. S. BUCHANAN joined the Coy & took up his appointment of 2nd in command.	
do	15 to 24		Training & Refitting	
do	25		Left FRANQUEVILLE & marched to BEAUVAL. The Company (less Transport) [illegible] proceeded to FORCEVILLE by [illegible]	
FORCEVILLE	26		Transport rejoined from BEAUVAL. 2/Lt W. D. LAWSON joined the Company	
do	27		LIEUT W. E. S. NAPIER left to assume duties as 2nd in command of No. 153 Coy M.G.C. The Company marched to HEDAUVILLE	

Army Form C. 2118.

WAR DIARY
or
INTELLIGENCE SUMMARY
(Erase heading not required.)

Instructions regarding War Diaries and Intelligence Summaries are contained in F. S. Regs., Part II. and the Staff Manual respectively. Title Pages will be prepared in manuscript.

SHEET →

74th M. G. COMPANY MACHINE GUN CORPS.

Place	Date	Hour	Summary of Events and Information	Remarks and references to Appendices
HEDAUVILLE	1916 Sep 27		(Later) The Company left HEDAUVILLE to relieve the 146 M.G. Coy in the THIEPVAL WOOD Sector. Casualties 5.	
THIEPVAL WOOD	28 & 29		The Company occupied positions in the trenches in THIEPVAL WOOD	
	30		Half-Company left trenches & marched to ENGELBELMER	

D. S. Buchanan Lt
a/ Commanding 74th M. G. Company
Capt.
Machine Gun Corps.

2449 Wt. W14957/M90 750,000 1/16 J.B.C. & A. Forms/C.2118/12.

74th Inf. Bde.

25th Division.

74th MACHINE GUN COY.,

O C T O B E R, 1 9 1 6.

October

Instructions regarding War Diaries and Intelligence Summaries are contained in F. S. Regs., Part II. and the Staff Manual respectively. Title pages will be prepared in manuscript.

WAR DIARY 25 or INTELLIGENCE SUMMARY.

(Erase heading not required.)

7th Coy Machine Gun Corps

Army Form C. 2118.

25

Vol. 6

Place	Date	Hour	Summary of Events and Information	Remarks and references to Appendices
	1916 Oct			
THIEPVAL WOOD	1		Half Company left ENGELBELMER & marched to BOUZINCOURT. The other Half-Coy remained in trenches at THIEPVAL WOOD & sustained 3 Casualties	
	2		The remaining Half Coy was relieved by 54 & 55 Coy M.G. C & marched to BOUZINCOURT.	
BOUZINCOURT	3/4		Training & refitting.	
	5		Occupied positions in HESSIAN Trench ZOLLERN Trench & MOUQUET FARM.	
MOUQUET FARM	9		Supported attack on STUFF REDOUBT by 7th Inf Bde & on REGINA TRENCH by Canadians.	
	16		Wire in front of REGINA Trench fired on to prevent repairs being made by enemy.	
	21		The Brigade attacked REGINA Trench from R23 A24 to R22 A38 2/Lt WILLIAMS was attached to 13th Cheshires with 2 guns 2/Lt MOGRIDGE was attached to 11th Lancs Fusiliers & 2/Lt MOSKOVITCH with 9th Loyal N. Lancs. The 2nd Royal Irish Rifles were holding HESSIAN trench 2/Lt LAWSON was attached to this Bn with 2 guns. Indirect fire was carried out by 8 guns from ZOLLERN EAST trench. Targets Sunken Road from R16C66 NW RAVINE to 11C18. High ground on R. of Ravine in 17A. 2/Lt WILLIAMS went over with 1st wave. He was killed in the first 20 yards. Sergt BISHOP carried on & got both guns mounted. 2/Lt MOSKOVITCH went over with second wave. He sustained several casualties from Snipers, but got both guns mounted. 2/Lt MOGRIDGE	

October

Instructions regarding War Diaries and Intelligence Summaries are contained in F. S. Regs., Part II. and the Staff Manual respectively. Title pages will be prepared in manuscript.

WAR DIARY
or
INTELLIGENCE SUMMARY.
(Erase heading not required.)

76 Coy Machine Gun Corps — 2 —

Army Form C. 2118.

Place	Date	Hour	Summary of Events and Information	Remarks and references to Appendices
	1916 Oct			
MOUQUET FARM	21 ctd		went over with the 3rd wave of 11th Lancs Fus. His party went too fast & formed our own barrage. 2/Lt MOBRIDGE was slightly wounded, but remained at duty. The enemy showed no desire to fight at close quarters. The Company obtained possession of two enemy machine guns & 1 automatic rifle. Total Casualties during tour Killed O. 1 OR 8 wounded O 2 OR. 25 missing O.R. 6.	
	22		Relieved by 55 Coy M.G.C. & marched to ALBERT.	
ALBERT	23		Marched to VADENCOURT.	
VADENCOURT	24		" BEAUVAL.	
BEAUVAL	25		Officers & men who participated in attack inspected by G.O.C. Reserve Army.	
	26		Coy inspected by G.O.C.-in-C. (Sir D. HAIG) & thanked. LT. D.S. BUCHANAN to England (leave) LT. W.A. RUTHERFORD assumed temporary command. LT. A.J. DICK reported for duty.	
	28		LT R. FARADAY reported for duty.	
	29		Left BEAUVAL & entrained at CANDAS.	
	30		Arrived at CAESTRE.	
	31		Training & Refitting	

W.A. Rutherford Lt ~~Capt.~~
Commanding 76th M. G. Company,
Machine Gun Corps.

T2134. Wt. W708–776. 500000. 4/15. Sir J. C. & S.

74th Inf. Bde.

25th Division

74th MACHINE GUN COY.,

N O V E M B E R, 1 9 1 6.

NOVEMBER

Instructions regarding War Diaries and Intelligence Summaries are contained in F. S. Regs., Part II. and the Staff Manual respectively. Title Pages will be prepared in manuscript.

WAR DIARY
or
~~INTELLIGENCE SUMMARY~~ 74 Coy M.G.C

(Erase heading not required.)

Army Form C. 2118.

Vol 7

Place	Date 1916	Hour	Summary of Events and Information	Remarks and references to Appendices
CAESTRE	Nov 1		Left CAESTRE & marched to METEREN.	
METEREN	2		" METEREN " NIEPPE	
NIEPPE	3		" NIEPPE & occupied the PLOEGSTEERT SECTOR Trenches	
PLOEGSTEERT	4 – 8		Trench Routine. LIEUT. R GARDNER joined for duty 4.11.16	
	9	10.30AM	Gas discharge by us.	
	10 – 26		Trench Routine. 2/LT. R.L.PARTON joined for duty 11.11.16	
	27		LIEUT N.F MARRIOTT joined for duty. Appointed C.O.	
	2[illegible]		LIEUT. D.S. BUCHANAN left for UK.	
	28 – 30		Trench Routine Casualties in action during month 1 OR Killed 1 O.R. wounded	

W.A. Rutherford Lt
for O.C. 74 Coy, M.G.C

2449 Wt. W14957/M90 750,000 1/16 J.B.C. & A. Forms/C.2118/12.

Instructions regarding War Diaries and Intelligence Summaries are contained in F. S. Regs., Part II. and the Staff Manual respectively. Title Pages will be prepared in manuscript.

WAR DIARY

-or-

~~INTELLIGENCE SUMMARY~~

(Erase heading not required.)

74th M G Coy.

Vol 9

Army Form C. 2118.

Place	Date	Hour	Summary of Events and Information	Remarks and references to Appendices
PLOEGSTEERT SECTOR.	1/1/17		Six teams from 195th Coy. Machine Gun Corps were attached to 74th M.G. Coy. today.	
28 S.W. 4 Edition 4A Scale 1/10000.]	9/1/17		During wire-cutting operation by artillery today 74th M.G. Coy. fired Indirect Enfilade Fire on ULTIMO LANE, ULTIMO AVENUE, ULTRA LANE, UMBO LANE and UMBO SUPPORT.	
	15/1/17		Lieut. H.F. MARRIOTT, M.C. to be Acting Captain, 11/12/16. Lieut. W.A. RUTHERFORD to be Acting Captain from 11/11/16 to 26/11/16.	
	17/1/17		There was a fall of snow late tonight.	
	18/1/17		Snow fell at intervals during the day. 74th M.G. Coy. took part in operations this afternoon firing on UMPIRE ROW and C.T.s between U 22 C. 45.00 and U 22 C. 25.40 from 2.5 pm to 3.20 pm, and at intervals during the night.	
	21/1/17		Keen frost set in today.	
	23/1/17		Enemy attacked this afternoon on a Five Division Front after bombarding our lines from 1.45 pm to 5.45 pm. Our casualties were four killed and three wounded.	
	31/1/17		Keen frost which commenced on 21/1/17 still continues.	

Instructions regarding War Diaries and Intelligence Summaries are contained in F. S. Regs., Part II. and the Staff Manual respectively. Title pages will be prepared in manuscript.

WAR DIARY
~~or~~
~~INTELLIGENCE SUMMARY.~~ 74th M.G. Coy.
(Erase heading not required.)

Army Form C. 2118.

VF10

Place	Date	Hour	Summary of Events and Information	Remarks and references to Appendices
PLOEGSTEERT SECTOR.	2/2/17		74th Coy. Machine Gun Corps was relieved today by 7th Coy Machine Gun Corps. 74th M.G. Coy. marched by HYDE PARK CORNER to camp at T.26 d.4.2. near DE SEULE. Relief was completed by 10 am. Hard frost still continues.	
	5/2/17		Six Gun Teams of 74th M.G. Coy. went on detachment to CAESTRE this morning to relieve Six Gun Teams of 2nd ANZACS. Relief was completed by 2 p.m. CAESTRE guns are to be used for anti-aircraft work.	
	9/2/17		Two guns from 74th M.G. Coy. took part with 2nd R.I. Rifles in a Battalion practice attack this forenoon from 9.30 - 1. Two more guns took part with 9th Loyal North Lancs. Regt. in a similar attack from 1 to 4.30 this afternoon.	
	10/2/17		74th M.G. Coy. took part in Brigade Route March today. First line transport accompanied units.	
	10/2/17		Lieut. GUSTAV FREDERICK WOLFF and 2/Lieut. JOSEPH ROSSITER from Machine Gun Corps Base Depôt reported for duty tonight.	
	11/2/17		Milder weather today. The frost still holds, but it is less severe today.	
	12/2/17		Two guns from 74th M.G. Coy. took part with 11th Lancashire Fusiliers in a Battalion practice attack this forenoon from 9.30 to 1. Two guns took part with 13th Cheshire	

T2134. Wt. W708–776. 500000. 4/15. Sir J. C. & S.

Instructions regarding War Diaries and Intelligence Summaries are contained in F. S. Regs., Part II. and the Staff Manual respectively. Title pages will be prepared in manuscript.

WAR DIARY
~~or~~
~~INTELLIGENCE SUMMARY.~~
(Erase heading not required.)

Army Form C. 2118.

Place	Date	Hour	Summary of Events and Information	Remarks and references to Appendices
			Regiment in a similar attack from 1 to 4.30 this afternoon.	
	13/2/17		74th Infantry Brigade practised a Brigade attack today. Eight guns from 74th M.G. Coy. took part.	
	13/2/17		Revolvers were issued to all ranks of 74th M.G. Company today, and all rifles were withdrawn.	
	14/2/17		74th M.G. Coy was inspected today by Brigadier-General BETHELL, commanding 74th Brigade, and Major DEANE DRUMMOND, Divisional Machine Gun Officer, 25th Division.	
	15/2/17		Two guns from 74th M.G. Coy. left late tonight for cross-roads at DE SEULE to be ready for anti-aircraft work.	
	16/2/17		Brigade Route March today was taken part in by 74th M.G. Coy. First line transport accompanied units. Hard frost again set in today.	
	17/2/17		Fresh weather set in today. Thaw restrictions were imposed today.	
	17/2/17		Eight guns and teams proceeded to PLOEGSTEERT WOOD today to take part in operation. There were no casualties, and an effective barrage of fire was maintained.	
	19/2/17		Brigade practised attack today. Two guns from 74th M.G. Coy. were attached to each battalion.	

Instructions regarding War Diaries and Intelligence Summaries are contained in F. S. Regs., Part II. and the Staff Manual respectively. Title pages will be prepared in manuscript.

WAR DIARY

~~or~~

~~INTELLIGENCE SUMMARY.~~

(*Erase heading not required.*)

Army Form C. 2118.

Place	Date	Hour	Summary of Events and Information	Remarks and references to Appendices
	19/2/17		Five men from each battalion in the 74th Infantry Brigade were attached to 74th M.G. Company today with a view to transfer.	
T26 d. 4. 2. CAESTRE.	20/2/17		74th M.G. Coy. left Camp at T26 d. 4. 2. this morning and marched by BAILLEUL to CAESTRE. Rain fell most of the way. There were no casualties. Two guns and their teams joined the company at DE SEULE en route.	
RENÉSCURE	21/2/17		74th M.G. Coy. marched today from CAESTRE to RENÉSCURE. There were no casualties on the march.	
ETRÉHEM.	22/2/17		Company marched today from RENÉSCURE to ETRÉHEM. There were no casualties on the march.	
ETRÉHEM	25/2/17		Staff Ride today was taken part in by O.C. 74th M.G. Coy.	
	26/2/17.		O.C. and 2nd I/C. 74th M.G. Coy. attended lecture at Artillery School, TILQUES today. Subject of lecture was, "Co-operation of Artillery and Infantry from an Infantry point of view."	
	26/2/17		The guns and teams on detachment at CAESTRE joined the company this afternoon. The whole company is now together.	
	27/2/17		All the officers and ten N.C.O's of full rank attended lectures at WISQUES	

Instructions regarding War Diaries and Intelligence Summaries are contained in F. S. Regs., Part II. and the Staff Manual respectively. Title pages will be prepared in manuscript.

WAR DIARY

~~or~~

~~INTELLIGENCE SUMMARY.~~

(Erase heading not required.)

Army Form C. 2118.

Place	Date	Hour	Summary of Events and Information	Remarks and references to Appendices
			today.	
	27/2/17	.	74th M.G. Coy, in charge of C.S.M. MARTIN, took part in Brigade Route march today. First line transport did not accompany units. Full marching order less great coats was carried, and there were no casualties in the company. The distance marched by the 74th M.G. Coy. was 24 Kilometres.	

T2134. Wt. W708-776. 500000. 4/15. Sir J. C. & S.

Instructions regarding War Diaries and Intelligence Summaries are contained in F. S. Regs., Part II. and the Staff Manual respectively. Title Pages will be prepared in manuscript.

WAR DIARY ~~or~~ ~~INTELLIGENCE~~ SUMMARY of 74th Bde M.G. Coy.

(Erase heading not required.)

Army Form C. 2118.

Vol. XI

Place	Date	Hour	Summary of Events and Information	Remarks and references to Appendices
ETRÉHEM	1/3/17		All officers and ten full ranks attended lectures at 2nd Army School, WISQUES today.	
	1/3/17		In future only C.O., 2nd I/c. and Section Officers will be mounted.	
	2/3/17		Staff Ride today taken part in by C.O. and 2nd I/C.	
	3/3/17		Football match today. Officers v. W.O., Staff Sergt. and sergeants. Result 6 – 0 in favour of officers.	
	4/3/17		Lieut. E.C. MOGRIDGE, 2nd I/C proceeded to course at 2nd Army School, WISQUES today. Lieut. A.J. DICK will act as 2nd I/C.	
			Football match today. 75th Field Ambulance v. 74th M.G. Company. Result 6 – 0 in favour of 75th Field Ambulance.	
	5/3/17		Snow fell during the night of 4/5 and continued till mid-day today.	
	6/3/17		Another fall of snow this morning.	
	7/3/17		Fall of snow today.	
	10/3/17		Brigade Operation was taken part in by 74th Machine Gun Company today. Company marched off at 7.18 am, and marched about 19 miles making an attack for about 4 miles across difficult country. Only one man fell out during the operations.	
	11/3/17		74th M.G. Coy. left ETRÉHEM at 12.40 p.m. today, and marched to CORNETTE.	

2449 Wt. W14957/M90 750,000 1/16 J.B.C. & A. Forms/C.2118/12.

Army Form C. 2118.

Instructions regarding War Diaries and Intelligence Summaries are contained in F. S. Regs., Part II. and the Staff Manual respectively. Title Pages will be prepared in manuscript.

WAR DIARY
or
INTELLIGENCE SUMMARY
(Erase heading not required.)

Place	Date	Hour	Summary of Events and Information	Remarks and references to Appendices
CORMETTE	14/3/17		All kits were reduced to regulation size today. Football match today between 9th Bn. Loyal North Lancashire Regt. and 74th M.G. Coy on ground of 9th L.N. Lancs. at ZUDAUSQUES. Result 3-1 in favour of 9th Bn Loyal North Lancashire Regt.	
	17/3/17		74th Infantry Brigade Marathon Race took place today. The race was won by 4581 Pte WILSON, J.H., 74th M.G. Coy. The second place was taken by 16880 L/Cpl KANE, R., and the third place by 42666 Pte KIRKPATRICK, T. Both these men also belonged to 74th M.G. Coy.	
	18/3/17		25th Divisional Artillery Show was held today at LUMBRES. The First Prize for limbered wagon was won by 74th M.G. Company.	
	20/3/17		74th M.G. Coy. left CORMETTE at 8 a.m. today, and marched by ETRÉHEM, WISQUES, WIZERNES and RENESCURE to WALLON-CAPPEL. The distance marched was 20 miles. Showers of snow fell during the latter part of the march. There were no casualties.	
WALLON-CAPPEL	21/3/17		74th M.G. Coy. marched from WALLON-CAPPEL today, by BORRÉ and PRADELLES to billets near STRAZEELE. Distance marched by Company was ten miles. There were no casualties. Showers of snow fell at intervals.	
STRAZEELE	22/3/17		74th M.G. Coy. as part of 25th Division is attached to 2nd Australian and New Zealand Army Corps from today.	

2449 Wt. W14957/M90 750,000 1/16 J.B.C. & A. Forms/C.2118/12.

Army Form C. 2118.

WAR DIARY
or
INTELLIGENCE SUMMARY

(Erase heading not required.)

Instructions regarding War Diaries and Intelligence Summaries are contained in F. S. Regs., Part II. and the Staff Manual respectively. Title Pages will be prepared in manuscript.

Place	Date	Hour	Summary of Events and Information	Remarks and references to Appendices
	29/3/17		74th M.G. Coy. left billets near STRAZEELE today and marched by STRAZEELE, BAILLEUL, NIEPPE and PONT DE NIEPPE to billets in ARMENTIÈRES. Distance marched was 15 miles. There were no casualties on the march. The Company reached ARMENTIÈRES at 2 P.M., and took over billets in the RUE NATIONALE.	
	31/3/17		Lieut. E.C MOGRIDGE rejoined company from 2nd Army School, WISQUES.	

Instructions regarding War Diaries and Intelligence Summaries are contained in F. S. Regs., Part II. and the Staff Manual respectively. Title Pages will be prepared in manuscript.

WAR DIARY
or
INTELLIGENCE SUMMARY
(Erase heading not required.)

Army Form C. 2118.

Vol 12

Place	Date	Hour	Summary of Events and Information	Remarks and references to Appendices
			74th Coy. Machine Gun Corps	
ARMENTIÈRES	1/4/17		Church Parade today.	
	2/4/17		Strengthening ARMENTIÈRES defences under 3rd Australian Pioneers. This work was continued until 5/4/17.	
	6/4/17		74th M.G. Coy. left ARMENTIÈRES this morning after being relieved by 10th M.G. Coy, A.I.F., and marched by DE SEULE to billets near STEENT-JE.	
STEENT-JE.	8/4/17		Heavy showers of snow fell during the day.	
	11/4/17		74th M.G. Coy. took part in Brigade Practice attack today.	
BULFORD CAMP	12/4/17		74th M.G. Coy. left billets at STEENT-JE this morning and marched to BULFORD CAMP on the NEUVE EGLISE road, relieving H.Q. 75th M.G. Coy. there. Nos. 3 and 4 sections of 74th M.G. Coy. proceeded to the trenches in WULVERGHEM Sector tonight, with advanced Coy H.Q. at SOUVENIR FARM, relieving 75th M.G. Coy.	
WULVERGHEM SECTOR.				
	15/4/17		Inter-section relief complete tonight.	
	17/4/17		Seven reinforcements joined the Company today	
	19/4/17		Inter-section relief complete tonight.	
	20/4/17		Captain N. F. MARRIOTT, M.C., Commanding 74th M.G. Coy. proceeded on leave to U.K. tonight	
	21/4/17		Inter-section relief complete tonight.	
	24/4/17		Inter-section relief complete tonight.	

2449 Wt. W14957/M90 750,000 1/16 J.B.C. & A. Forms/C.2118/12.

Army Form C. 2118.

WAR DIARY
or
INTELLIGENCE SUMMARY
(Erase heading not required.)

Instructions regarding War Diaries and Intelligence Summaries are contained in F. S. Regs., Part II. and the Staff Manual respectively. Title Pages will be prepared in manuscript.

Place	Date	Hour	Summary of Events and Information	Remarks and references to Appendices
WULVERGHEM SECTOR.	24/4/17		No. 60201 Pte McFARLANE, D. was killed in action at SHELL FARM tonight.	
LA CRÊCHE.	27/4/17		74th M.G. Coy. was relieved today by 195th M.G. Coy, and came back to billets at village of LA CRÊCHE.	
	28/4/17		No. 72821 Pte KENYON, E. was accidentally killed in billets today by bullet from rifle.	
	29/4/17		Baggage wagon from 199th Coy. A.S.C. joined Company tonight	
	30/4/17		74th M.G. Coy. carried out a practice attack today at the MONT DE LILLE.	
	30/4/17		Company Transport moved from WACKLANDS CAMP to LA CRÊCHE.	
	30/4/17		Strength of Company: 11 Officers and 210 Other Ranks, including 32 men attached from battalion. There are 9 Other Ranks in hospital.	

74th M.G. COMPANY
1/5/17
MACHINE GUN CORPS

Lieut.
for Commanding 74th M. G. Coy.
Machine Gun Corps.

2449 Wt. W14957/M90 750,000 1/16 J.B.C. & A. Forms/C.2118/12.

Instructions regarding War Diaries and Intelligence Summaries are contained in F. S. Regs., Part II. and the Staff Manual respectively. Title pages will be prepared in manuscript.

WAR DIARY
or
INTELLIGENCE SUMMARY.
(Erase heading not required.)

Army Form C. 2118.

Vol / 3

Place	Date	Hour	Summary of Events and Information	Remarks and references to Appendices
			74th Company, Machine Gun Corps.	
LA CRÊCHE	1.5.17		The fine weather of the past three days still continues.	
	2.5.17		Capt. N.F MARRIOTT, O.C. Company returned from leave to U.K. today. Lecture tonight by B.G.C. to all officers and full rank.	
	3.5.17		The Company was inspected today on Training Ground at MONT DE LILLE. All the attached men were returned to their battalions tonight, and were replaced by twenty-four others.	
	4.5.17		Attack practice at MONT DE LILLE.	
	5.5.17		Attack practice at MONT DE LILLE.	
BULFORD CAMP WULVERGHEM SECTOR.	9.5.17		Company left LA CRÊCHE this morning, and marched to BULFORD CAMP, relieving the 1st New Zealand M.G. Coy. there. At 12.30 pm three sections proceeded to the WULVERGHEM SECTOR, and relieved the 1st N.Z. M.G. Coy.	
	13.5.17		Seven guns of the Company engaged NUTMEG AVENUE, NUTMEG LANE, Communication Trenches south of the latter and UGLY RESERVE with enfilade fire between 5 and 5.45 pm in conjunction with the artillery. During the night Machine Guns co-operated with Lewis Guns and Patrols to prevent enemy mending his wire.	
	15.5.17		Inter-section relief took place tonight. Rain fell today — the first this month.	

T.2134. Wt. W708-776. 500000. 4/15. Sir J. C. & S.

Instructions regarding War Diaries and Intelligence Summaries are contained in F. S. Regs., Part II. and the Staff Manual respectively. Title pages will be prepared in manuscript.

WAR DIARY
or
INTELLIGENCE SUMMARY.
(Erase heading not required.)

Army Form C. 2118.

Place	Date	Hour	Summary of Events and Information	Remarks and references to Appendices
	16.5.17		In co-operation with the infantry operations two guns barraged immediately east of NUTMEG RESERVE, one gun barraged NUTMEG AVENUE, and one from N 36 d 75.03 to O 31 c.10.13 (Sheet 28 S.W.), and eleven guns barraged from O 32 C central to O 31 b central (Sheet 28 S.W.)	
	21.5.17		Inter-section relief today. 2/Lieut. A.F.M. BERKELEY from M.G. Base Depôt reported for duty today.	
	22.5.17		Two reinforcements arrived from M.G. Base Depôt today.	
	25.5.17		74th M.G. Coy. left BULFORD CAMP this morning after relief by 7th M.G. Coy. and marched	
RAVELSBERG			to RAVELSBERG where the sections from the WULVERGHEM SECTOR joined the Company after being relieved by 7th M.G. Coy. Company then marched to BAILLEUL and entrained for WATTEN. From WATTEN Company marched to billets in village of LA	
LA RECOUSSE.			RECOUSSE. The warm weather still continues.	
	26.5.17		Practice attack by Brigade this forenoon. 74th M.G. Coy. took part. Brigade bivouacked all night on training ground.	
	27.5.17		Practice attack repeated at dawn.	
	28.5.17		Practice attack repeated today.	

T2134. Wt. W708-776. 500000. 4/15. Sir J. C. & S.

Instructions regarding War Diaries and Intelligence Summaries are contained in F. S. Regs., Part II. and the Staff Manual respectively. Title pages will be prepared in manuscript.

WAR DIARY
or
INTELLIGENCE SUMMARY.
(Erase heading not required.)

Army Form C. 2118.

Place	Date	Hour	Summary of Events and Information	Remarks and references to Appendices
	29.5.17		Company left LA RECOUSSE today and entrained at WATTEN for BAILLEUL. Marched from	
LA CRÊCHE.			BAILLEUL to billets near village of LA CRÊCHE.	
	31.5.17		Six men of the Company and six attached men – all in hospital – were struck off strength today by authority of A.D.M.S. 25th Division. Twenty men from battalions in the Brigade were attached as a carrying party today. One other rank joined as a reinforcement from M.G. Base Depôt.	
	31.5.17		Strength of Company on this date:–	
			12 Officers	
			224 Other Ranks (including 46 attached)	
			5 Other Ranks in hospital.	

[signature] Lieut
for O/Commanding 74th M.G. Company,
Machine Gun Corps.

T2134. Wt. W708–776. 500000. 4/15. Sir J. C. & S.

Instructions regarding War Diaries and Intelligence Summaries are contained in F. S. Regs., Part II. and the Staff Manual respectively. Title Pages will be prepared in manuscript.

WAR DIARY
or
INTELLIGENCE SUMMARY
(Erase heading not required.)

Army Form C. 2118.

74 M G Coy

Vol 14

Place	Date	Hour	Summary of Events and Information	Remarks and references to Appendices
			74th Coy. Machine Gun Corps.	
LA CRÊCHE	1/6/17		The fine weather still continues.	
	2/6/17		Lecture this forenoon to all officers and full ranks by Col APPLIN, Corps Machine Gun Officer	
	3/6/17		Church Parade. Company afterwards inspected model of MESSINES RIDGE. For the past few days the enemy has shewn considerable aeroplane activity. He has also shelled back areas including BAILLEUL and STEENT-JE.	
	4/6/17		Captain MARRIOTT, M.C. attended C.O's Conference at Brigade H.Q. today.	
BREEMEERSCHEN	5/6/17		Company moved today to ~~billets~~ bivouacs at BREEMEERSCHEN.	
WULVERGHEM SECTOR	6/6/17		Company left BREEMEERSCHEN this afternoon, and marched to places in Assembly Trenches in the WULVERGHEM SECTOR. Enemy shelled back areas including NEUVE ÉGLISE today. One man was wounded in 74th Company. The disposition of the Company was as follows:-	
			Eight guns assembled in O.B.1 and FUSILIER TRENCH, six guns took up positions for barrage fire, and two guns went to Brigade H.Q.	
			During the night of 6th/7th June the enemy sent over several gas shells	
	7/6/17		At ZERO (3.10 a.m.) the Brigade attacked. Four guns of 74th M.G. Coy. left the Assembly Trenches, three of which came into action about NUTMEG RESERVE. Most of the team of the other gun were put out of action. Lieut. R. FARADAY and 2/Lieut. A.F.H. BERKELEY were killed by a shell about 3 a.m. Lieut. R. GARDNER was wounded soon after leaving the Assembly Trench	

2449 Wt. W14957/M90 750,000 1/16 J.B.C. & A. Forms/C.2118/12.

Instructions regarding War Diaries and Intelligence Summaries are contained in F. S. Regs., Part II. and the Staff Manual respectively. Title Pages will be prepared in manuscript.

WAR DIARY
or
INTELLIGENCE SUMMARY
(Erase heading not required.)

Army Form C. 2118.

Place	Date	Hour	Summary of Events and Information	Remarks and references to Appendices
WULVERGHEM SECTOR.	7/6/17		At ZERO + 20 minutes the remaining four guns left the Assembly Trenches, and got into action in and about OCTOBER SUPPORT at about ZERO + 2 hours with slight casualties.	
			At ZERO + 2½ hours the guns at NUTMEG RESERVE moved up to reinforce the guns at OCTOBER SUPPORT.	
			At ZERO + 2 hours the two guns in Brigade Reserve moved to OCTOBER SUPPORT arriving there about ZERO + 3 hours.	
			At ZERO + 4 hours there were nine guns in action in and about OCTOBER SUPPORT These guns at once dug in.	
			At ZERO + 1 hour 50 minutes the barrage guns moved forward to positions about one hundred yards east of the MESSINES - WYTSCHAETE ROAD and prepared for an S.O.S. barrage on ~~OCTOBER~~ OWL SUPPORT and ODIOUS SUPPORT. 2/Lieut R.L. PARTON was wounded here.	
			At ZERO + 10 hours 10 minutes these guns opened fire on their barrage lines, and rolled back 500 yards at the rate of 50 yards per minute, then firing for 10 minutes and ceasing fire. The guns remained ready to open fire again on the S.O.S. going up.	
	8/6/17		Four guns were withdrawn to Old British Line. Emplacements were improved	
	9/6/17		Three guns were withdrawn to NUTMEG RESERVE. Guns from Old British Line moved to NUTMEG RESERVE. Eight guns remained in action about OCTOBER SUPPORT.	

2449 Wt. W14957/M90 750,000 1/16 J.B.C. & A. Forms/C.2118/12.

Instructions regarding War Diaries and Intelligence Summaries are contained in F. S. Regs., Part II. and the Staff Manual respectively. Title Pages will be prepared in manuscript.

WAR DIARY
or
INTELLIGENCE SUMMARY
(Erase heading not required.)

Army Form C. 2118.

Place	Date	Hour	Summary of Events and Information	Remarks and references to Appendices
DRANOUTRE.	11/6/17		The Company was withdrawn today to bivouacs on the NEUVE ÉGLISE – DRANOUTRE ROAD.	
			Casualties during operations from 7/6/17 to 11/6/17 inclusive were as follows:-	
			Killed. 2 officers and 7 O.R.	
			Wounded 2 officers and 32 O.R.	
	12/6/17		"B" Team and 28 reinforcements arrived today from MORBECQUE.	
MESSINES RIDGE.	13/6/17		Eight teams went back to the line today.	
	15/6/17		These teams were relieved and returned to bivouacs on NEUVE ÉGLISE - DRANOUTRE ROAD.	
DRANOUTRE.	16/6/17		74th Brigade Sports were held today.	
MESSINES RIDGE.	17/6/17		Company went into the line tonight at a part of the line more to the right than last time.	
			2/Lieut. W. L. JOHNSTONE, 2/Lieut. W. BOWLER and 2/Lieut. T. L. CLARKE reported for duty with Company today. Reinforcement of 7 men arrived from M.G. Base Depôt today.	
	18/6/17		Reinforcement of 4 men arrived today from M.G. Base Depôt.	
	23/6/17		Company was relieved early this morning by 11th Australian M.G. Coy. Great aerial activity was displayed by enemy during this tour in the line. Company marched to Transport Lines on WULVERGHEM – NEUVE ÉGLISE . ROAD. Left there by motor-bus this morning and proceeded by NEUVE ÉGLISE, ESTAIRES and MERVILLE	

2449 Wt. W14957/M90 750,000 1/16 J.B.C. & A. Forms/C.2118/12.

Army Form C. 2118.

Instructions regarding War Diaries and Intelligence Summaries are contained in F. S. Regs., Part II. and the Staff Manual respectively. Title Pages will be prepared in manuscript.

WAR DIARY
or
INTELLIGENCE SUMMARY
(Erase heading not required.)

Place	Date	Hour	Summary of Events and Information	Remarks and references to Appendices
CAUDESCURE			In billets in CAUDESCURE. 2/Lieut. ROSSITER and Cpl. CHALCROFT remained behind to represent the company at the inspection by H.R.H. the Duke of Connaught.	
HAM-EN-ARTOIS	24/6/17		Company left CAUDESCURE tonight and marched by ST. VENANT to HAM-EN-ARTOIS.	
ESTRÉE BLANCHE.	25/6/17		Left HAM-EN-ARTOIS tonight and marched to ESTRÉE BLANCHE.	
HEZECQUES	26/6/17		Left ESTRÉE BLANCHE tonight and marched by CUHEM to HEZECQUES.	
	27/6/17		Lieut A J DICK and 2 O.R. proceeded on leave to U.K today.	
	27/6/17		72812 Pte WALSH, T. awarded the Military Medal.	
	28/6/17		Lieut.-General JACOB, commanding 2nd Corps met officers of 74th Brigade today.	
	29/6/17		2/Lieut J ROSSITER awarded the Military Cross, and 6819 Cpl C. CHALCROFT awarded the Military Medal.	
	29/6/17		One reinforcement arrived from M.G. Base Depôt today.	
	30/6/17		Total casualties since 7th June, 1917:- Killed 2 officers 10 O.R Wounded 2 officers 34 O.R Strength of Company is as follows:- 12 officers (including 1 posted but not yet joined) 205 O.R. (including 28 attached) 4 O.Rs are in hospital.	

for [signature] Lieut
Capt.
Commanding 74th M. G. Company,
Machine Gun Corps.

2449 Wt. W14957/M90 750,000 1/16 J.B.C. & A. Forms/C.2118/12.

Instructions regarding War Diaries and Intelligence Summaries are contained in F. S. Regs., Part II. and the Staff Manual respectively. Title Pages will be prepared in manuscript.

WAR DIARY
or
INTELLIGENCE SUMMARY
(Erase heading not required.)

Army Form C. 2118.

Vol 15

Place	Date	Hour	Summary of Events and Information	Remarks and references to Appendices
			74th Company Machine Gun Corps.	
HEZECQUES	1.7.17		Church Parades and general cleaning up today.	
	2.7.17		Names for "B" teams forwarded to Bde HQ. today.	
	3.7.17		Two attached men were returned to their units today, and thirty-six joined from battalions after inspection by B.G.C.	
			Route march from 9 am. to 12.30 pm today by MATRINGHEM, and VINCLY. Very warm day. Bathing parade this afternoon.	
			Two drivers arrived tonight, reinforcements from A.H.T. Depôt.	
	4.7.17		Heavy rain today, the first for several weeks.	
	5.7.17		A/Sergt LAMBOURNE rejoined from Base Depôt tonight.	
	6.7.17		Route march by MATRINGHEM, VINCLY, BEAUMETZ-LEZ-AIRE this forenoon. Bathing parade this afternoon. During the time the Company has been in HEZECQUES bathing has been indulged in frequently by the men.	
	9.7.17		Brigade practice attack today. Company marched out from billets at 10.30 pm.	
	10.7.17		Reached training ground at 1 am. Attack commenced at 3 am and finished at 4 am, march home at 9.30 am.	
	12.7.17		Brigade practice attack from 12.7.17 to 14.7.17.	
	12.7.17		Lieut. L. E. FABER, M.C. from 195th Company reported for duty today.	
	16.7.17		Brigade practice attack from 16/7/17 to 18/7/17.	

2449 Wt. W14957/M90 750,000 1/16 J.B.C. & A. Forms/C.2118/12.

Instructions regarding War Diaries and Intelligence Summaries are contained in F. S. Regs., Part II. and the Staff Manual respectively. Title Pages will be prepared in manuscript.

WAR DIARY
or
INTELLIGENCE SUMMARY
(Erase heading not required.)

Army Form C. 2118.

Place	Date	Hour	Summary of Events and Information	Remarks and references to Appendices
	16.7.17		Lieut. L.E. FABER, M.C. assumed command of company today.	
	17.7.17		Capt. N.F. MARRIOTT, M.C. proceeded to England today.	
	18.7.17		2/Lieut. O.W. WALDRON reported for duty today.	
			Lieut. E.C. MOGRIDGE and two N.C.Os proceeded to ABEELE today for course of aerial observation	
	20.7.17		Practice in the Training Area from 20.7.17 to 21.7.17	
	21.7.17		Lieut. R.J. DAVIES reported for duty today.	
WALLON-CAPPEL.	24.7.17		Company left HEZECQUES at 9.15 am and marched to MATRINGHEM, thence to EBBLINGHEM by motor-bus, and thence marched to billets near WALLON-CAPPEL.	
HONDEGHEM	25.7.17		Lieut. G.F. WOLFF appointed A/2nd I/C. of Company. Company marched this morning to HONDEGHEM	
EECKE.	26.7.17		Company marched this morning to billets near EECKE. Sixty-eight other ranks proceeded to PIONEER CAMP at 12 noon today.	
GODEWAERS-VELDE	27.7.17		Company marched this morning to billets near GODEWAERSVELDE. C.S.M. MARTIN rejoined from Base Depôt today. Eleven other ranks joined as reinforcements from Base Depôt today. Lieut. MOGRIDGE and two N.C.Os rejoined from Course at ABEELE. ~~Lieut. J. ROSSITER, M.C. proceeded to CAMIERS for Vickers Gun Course today.~~	

2449 Wt. W14957/M90 750,000 1/16 J.B.C. & A. Forms/C.2118/12.

Instructions regarding War Diaries and Intelligence Summaries are contained in F. S. Regs., Part II. and the Staff Manual respectively. Title pages will be prepared in manuscript.

WAR DIARY
or
INTELLIGENCE SUMMARY.
(Erase heading not required.)

Army Form C. 2118.

Place	Date	Hour	Summary of Events and Information	Remarks and references to Appendices
GODEVAERSVELDE. K35 c 05 Sh/27	28/7/17		Coy parade & inspection. Training of Coy continued. Mechanism I.A. & Gun drill. 2Lt ALDERBRUCE returned from front line. O.C. Coy & 2Lt WALDRON reconnoitred front area roads & tracks Sh 28 1/20000 H.23 & 24 I.13, 14, 15, 16 & 19. Lt. E.G. MOGRIDGE proceeded to HESDIN this am.; Sgt J. ROSSITER & Cpl proceeded to CAMIERS for M.G. Course. Weather fine. Coy played 13th Bn Cheshires at Cricket & won by 3 runs.	[illegible]
" "	29/7/17		Church Parades – cancelled owing to heavy Thunderstorm. Cleared later. "B" team proceeded this pm to OUDERZEELE. OC attended Bde conference.	[illegible]
" "	30/7/17		Coy parade cancelled owing to rain. Cleared in P.M. Coy taken [illegible] under 2Lt WOODRUFF. Officers studied maps & air photos of attack area. Carrying party under 2Lt JOHNSTONE returned from front line no casualties. At 5.30 pm transport under Lt LAWSON proceeded to forward area [illegible] in Sheet 28 1/20000 H22 in detachments by march route. Coy proceeded at 6.25 pm by march route to Sh 28. G17 d 31. Arrived 9.30 pm. 2Lt WALDRON billeting officer met Coy at BUSSEBOOM. 2Lt WOODRUFF to UK on leave.	[illegible]
Sheet 28 1/20000 G d 31.	31/7/17		Coy Parade at 9 am. Lt A. DICK, 2Lt T.L. CLARKE & barrage guns returned from front line at 11 am. Casualties 1 Killed (L/Cpl GRAHAM) & 4 wounded. 3 guns damaged. Lt. DICK praises work done by Sgts NUTT & RONALD. Guns fired from ZERO (3.50 am) till 5.05 am – 48000 rounds. Received orders from Bde to send a barrage battery of 8 guns up the line on morning of 1.8.17.	Gun Positions ZILLEBEKE 1/10000 I.21.a. 15.60 – 15 [illegible] Targets J.d.15.75 [illegible] ZONNEBEKE 1/10000 [illegible] J.1a.77.47 J.1.b.10.70.

T2134. Wt. W708–776. 500000. 4/15. Sir J. C. & S.

Instructions regarding War Diaries and Intelligence Summaries are contained in F. S. Regs., Part II, and the Staff Manual respectively. Title pages will be prepared in manuscript.

WAR DIARY
or
INTELLIGENCE SUMMARY.
(*Erase heading not required.*)

Army Form C. 2118.

Vol 16

Place	Date	Hour	Summary of Events and Information	Remarks and references to Appendices
			74th COMPANY MACHINE GUN CORPS.	
DOMINION CAMP Sheet 28 1/20000 G.17.d.3.1	1.8.17		Coy. Parade cancelled owing to heavy rain. Rain all preceding night & all day.	
			"A" Battery comprising Lt DAVIES 2Lt WALDRON 3 NCOs & 64 men 4 guns under Command	
			of Lt E F WOLFE proceeded on duty up the line 4 am. Lt Wolfe Davies 2Lt Waldron	
			& 3 NCOs & 2 orderlies reported to the DMGO at HALFWAY HO. at 4 am. Lt LAWSON	
			& 2Lt BOWLER took remainder of party to HALFWAY HO & reached there at 6 am. Lt	
			LAWSON returning with limbers leaving 2Lt BOWLER to report. D.M.G.O ordered	
I.12.b.3.7.		8pm	4 guns to be mounted on S.O.S. lines that afternoon. This was done but	
			with very great difficulty. Ground very heavy owing to constant rain	
			Guns heavily shelled all night but no casualties. 4 guns & teams in reserve	(at HALFWAY HOUSE)
	2.8.17		Still raining & ground becoming impassable near old British front line.	
			Gun teams relieved at 6 am & arrangements made for relief every 24 hrs.	
H.21.b.2.3			Remainder of Coy move to PIONEER CAMP & stand to.	
	3.8.17		Still raining. C.O. visits guns on positions & teams at HALFWAY HOUSE	
	4.8.17		"A" Battery under Lt WOLFE relieved by 2/Lts MACKRELL, JOHNSTONE & CLARKE	
			& 8 gun teams. Relief completed by 7.30 am. No casualties during "A" Battery's tour	
I.19.c.3.7			Coy move to SWAN CHATEAU. Transport return to old lines H.22.c.3.3.	

D. D. & L., London, E.C.
(A7883) Wt W809/M1672 350,000 4/17 Sch. 52a Forms/C/2118/14

Instructions regarding War Diaries and Intelligence Summaries are contained in F. S. Regs., Part II, and the Staff Manual respectively. Title pages will be prepared in manuscript.

WAR DIARY
or
INTELLIGENCE SUMMARY.
(Erase heading not required.)

Army Form C. 2118.

Place	Date	Hour	Summary of Events and Information	Remarks and references to Appendices
SHAN CHATEAU I 19.c.37 (contd.)	4.8.17		"A" Battery rejoin Coy at about 11am.	
	5.8.17		C.O. proceeds up the line at 3.30am. 8 guns at HALFWAY HOUSE take over	
			positions in front & support lines from 7th Coy. At 2pm remainder of Coy	
H.21.b.8.4.			under Lt WOLFF move back to PIONEER CAMP. Weather fine. Forward H.Q. at J7a 3510	(HOOGE 1/10000)
	6.8.17		Gun dispositions in front line as follows :- 4 guns under 2Lt MACKRELL at J7c 35-80 85-90 95.	
			2 guns under 2Lt Johnstone at J7c 80-80-95 & 2 guns under 2Lt CLARKE at J7d 7085	
			The night of 5/6 was marked by heavy shelling & gas. The guns & teams under 2Lt MACKRELL	
			suffered severely so the 4 guns were removed to J7a 30-10 15 20 25. New emplacements &	
			slit trenches were dug. 2nd Lt Johnstone's teams had a deep dug out. 2Lt CLARKE's ditto.	
			The two guns of the latter were engaged the night of 5/6th during a [illegible] attack of WIND.	
	7.8.17		Lt DAVIES, 2Lt WALDRON & BOWLER & teams relieve officers & men in the line. 2Lt WALDRON	
			taking over the command of the 4 guns on BELLEWARDE RIDGE. Relief completed 10am	
			The shelling continues to be very heavy - an enemy barrage came down as usual at 9 pm	
	8.8.17		preparations for following days attack completed - 20,000 rds SAA & 40 extra belt boxes	filled
			brought to BELLEWARDE RIDGE. 2 days rations [illegible]. The operation orders	
			were as follows. The 4 guns under 2Lt WALDRON were to put up a barrage on	

D. D. & L., London, E.C.
(A7883) Wt W809/M1672 350,000 4/17 Sch. 52a Forms/C/2118/14

Instructions regarding War Diaries and Intelligence Summaries are contained in F. S. Regs., Part II, and the Staff Manual respectively. Title pages will be prepared in manuscript.

WAR DIARY
or
INTELLIGENCE SUMMARY.
(*Erase heading not required.*)

Army Form C. 2118.

Place	Date	Hour	Summary of Events and Information	Remarks and references to Appendices
	8.8.17		ZONNEBEKE REDOUBT & J3a.0080.0580.1085.1585.2090. & fire from Zero to Zero + 1hr 30 mins. On Infantry gaining objective (Black Line WESTHOEK RIDGE) to go forward & consolidate on an eight point.	
			The 4 guns under Lt Davies with Sgt Bowler were to push forward & cover our right flank from direction of NONNE BOSCHEN during the attack (To do this they had to cross the WESTHOEK RIDGE) 2 of these guns however were to watch our flank closely as there was a likelihood of the division on our right being held up at GLENCORSE WOOD owing to rain Zero hour was postponed. The shelling continued day & night with intermittent barrage & S.O.S. fire thrown in.	
	9.8.17		This day was spent in anxious expectation.	
	10.8.17		We attacked at 4.35 am. The 4 guns under Lt Davies never got away. Lt DAVIES himself being wounded & guns knocked out. At 2 hrs 30 mins after Zero Sgt WALDRON had 2 guns on our right flank which was open & did splendid work there for the 30 hrs they were there. They fired 10500 rds & Sgt LAMBOURNE had 17500 rds brought up to these guns during that time. all of which, except 500 rds being in belt boxes.	
			1 gun under Sgt RONALD took up a position at J1d.9075 in the front of the	

D. D. & L., London, E.C.
(A7883) Wt W809/M1672 350,000 4/17 Sch. 52a. Forms/C/2118/14

Instructions regarding War Diaries and Intelligence Summaries are contained in F. S. Regs., Part II, and the Staff Manual respectively. Title pages will be prepared in manuscript.

WAR DIARY
or
INTELLIGENCE SUMMARY.
(Erase heading not required.)

Army Form C. 2118.

Place	Date	Hour	Summary of Events and Information	Remarks and references to Appendices
			9th Bn Loyal North Lancs Regt. who did very fine work. A little later in the	
			morning another gun was mounted at J8c9075	
	11.8.17		2Lt MACKRELL & 2Lt CLARKE relieved 2Lt WALDRON & teams – the latter however took one	
			the 4 new guns brought up & placed on BELLEWARDE RIDGE.	
			2Lt CLARKE took over the guns on the left* & 2Lt MACKRELL had 3 guns on the SNOUT⊕	* J8c8020
			2 mounted & 1 in deep dugout. The Coy now had eleven guns in the line & all that	⊕ J7d7080
			was left of its personnel. 2Lt WALDRON returned to billets in order to proceed to	(HOOGE 1/10000)
			IInd Army Central School of Instruction.	
	12.8.17		Lt WOLFE this am relieved CO. who returned to PIONEER CAMP.	
	13.8.17		The entire Coy was relieved by 2pm & were in billets at that time.	
			The Coy did exceedingly well on the whole during its tour. But our casualties were	
			heavy (1 officer killed 2 wounded & 1 gassed) viz 2Lt BOWLER killed Lt DAVIES & 2Lt	
			CLARKE wounded & 2Lt Johnstone gassed. 75 O R 15 killed 58 wounded 2 missing×	× includes attached men.
			Lt LAWSON brought up the ammn & rations splendidly in spite of enemy shelling.	
			2Lt WALDRON proceeded this AM to WISQUES to IInd Army Central School of Instruction	
			Coy bathed & issued with new clothing. 2Lt WOODRUFF returned from leave.	

D. D. & L., London, E.C.
(A7883) Wt W809/M1672 350,000 4/17 Sch. 52a Forms/C/2118/14

Instructions regarding War Diaries and Intelligence Summaries are contained in F. S. Regs., Part II. and the Staff Manual respectively. Title pages will be prepared in manuscript.

WAR DIARY
or
INTELLIGENCE SUMMARY.
(Erase heading not required.)

Army Form C. 2118.

Place	Date	Hour	Summary of Events and Information	Remarks and references to Appendices
H21284	14.8.17		Coy moved to billets in STEENVOORDE area.	
	15.8.17		refitting.	
	16.8.17		training.	
	17.8.17		moved to billets in EECKE area. 2nd Lt F.W. STEADMAN reported for duty.	
	18.8.17		training. Coy. strength 251 all ranks	
	19.8.17		Church parade [illegible] HQ 8th Bn Cheshire Regt.	
	20.8.17	8 am	moved to new billets in STEENVOORDE area. One farm very cramped - no officers billets ½ Coy. bivouaking. Weather fine. 2nd Lts T.H. MARSHALL + W WELDRICK reported for duty.	
Sheet 27 (1/40000) J24a 2015	21.8.17	9 am	rehearsed parade for inspection by C.I.C. who inspected the Bde this afternoon. The C.I.C. spent much time with us & spoke of the fine work this Coy had done & told the C.O. to convey his thanks to all ranks in this Coy. in fact one might say it was our day. (fine)	
"	22.8.17		Training of attached men & Coy proceeded. fine. 4 AA guns mtd. [illegible] of 9 [illegible]	
"	23.8.17		Training continued - Section scheme at K32 b 80 20. All officers + 40 O.R. attended a lecture by Capt. BLES. on "The Strategy of the War" at STEENVOORDE. Excellent lecture.	
	24.8.17		Training continued. billets at K32 b 80 20 fine.	
	25.8.17		Training continued. New guns tuned up on range. afternoon baths. Coy strength 255 A.R. 2nd ROSSITER + L S/I Trafford returned from CAMIERS.	

D. D. & L., London, E.C. (A7883) Wt W809/M1672 350,000 4/17 Sch. 52a Forms/C/2118/14

Instructions regarding War Diaries and Intelligence Summaries are contained in F. S. Regs., Part II, and the Staff Manual respectively. Title pages will be prepared in manuscript.

WAR DIARY
or
INTELLIGENCE SUMMARY.
(Erase heading not required.)

Army Form C. 2118.

Place	Date	Hour	Summary of Events and Information	Remarks and references to Appendices
Sheet 27 1/40000 J24a 2015	26.8.17		Fine. CHURCH PARADES. C of E 12.15pm. Own parade ground.	
			R.C. STEENVOORDE PARISH CHURCH 11.30am	
			Pres & N.Cs " 10am.	
			Rained all night 8/9th	
	27.8.17		Programme of WORK for week:-	
			8.45am DAILY. Company Parade. - Friday with Transport.	
			9.15-10am " Physical Training under 2nd Lt Rossiter M.C. (except Friday)	FRIDAY Whole day. Company Scheme at K.32 b. 80.20. (Sheet 27)
			10-11 RANGE + INSTRUCTION F24c35.	
			10-11.45am Monday & Tuesday LECTURE ALLOCATION of Duties. Wednesday & Thursday LECTURE FIRE DIRECTION (except Friday)	
			11.45-12.30 Monday & Tuesday Gun Drill. Wednesday & Thursday Limber Drill " "	Includes Mobility - men on limbers coming into action.
			2-3 pm DAILY C.S.M.s PARADE Squad & Arms Drill - Guards & Sentries - Saluting drill.	S.A.A. Depôts to be formed.
			9.15-1.30pm MONDAY - No 1&2 Sections. TUESDAY - No 3 & 4 Sections. Scheme at K.32 b 80.20. Includes Advancing with Pack Animals. Training of Ground Scouts & Runners. Training of Range TAKERS. DIGGING.	S.A.A. Brought up to guns etc.
			9.15-1.30pm WEDNESDAY - Nos 1 & 2 Sections. THURSDAY Nos 3 & 4 Sections. Scheme at K32 b 80.20. Includes - Gas drill. Indication and Recognition. Quick engaging of moving targets. Map Reading for Scouts & N.C.O's. Indirect Overhead Fire.	
			Saturday. Cleaning up Guns - Limbers etc.	

D. D. & L. London, E.C.
(A7883) Wt W809/M1672 350,000 4/17 Sch. 52a Forms/C/2118/14

Instructions regarding War Diaries and Intelligence Summaries are contained in F. S. Regs., Part II. and the Staff Manual respectively. Title pages will be prepared in manuscript.

WAR DIARY

or

~~INTELLIGENCE SUMMARY.~~

(Erase heading not required.)

Army Form C. 2118.

Place	Date	Hour	Summary of Events and Information	Remarks and references to Appendices
Sheet 27 1/40000 J24a 20.15.	27.8.17		owing to wet ground - section [illegible] a ROUTEMARCH.	
	28.8.17 to 31.8.17		Programme adhered to as far as possible but outdoor work hindered by wet weather. 31.8.17. Capt L.E.FABER M.C. & Sergt Lambourne left the Coy for a three weeks course at CAMIERES.	

Capt.
Commanding 74th M. G. Company,
Machine Gun Corps.

D. D. & L., London, E.C.
(A7883) Wt W809/M1672 350,000 4/17 Sch. 52a Forms/C/2118/14

25

Instructions regarding War Diaries and Intelligence Summaries are contained in F. S. Regs., Part II. and the Staff Manual respectively. Title pages will be prepared in manuscript.

WAR DIARY
or
INTELLIGENCE SUMMARY.
(Erase heading not required.)

Army Form C. 2118.

74th Coy

5

Vol 17

Place	Date	Hour	Summary of Events and Information	Remarks and references to Appendices
G 24 Central Sheet 28 NW.	1/9/17		Company moved to billets at G 24 C central (Sheet 28 NW) and remained one night 1/2nd. 2/9/17 Sections 3 & 4 with 8 guns commanded by 2/Lts T.H. MARSHALL	
	2/9/17		& W. WELDRICK respectively proceeded up the line to relieve the 142nd M.G. Coy 5 guns were relieved & 3 other guns were placed in positions sited by	
J1d3.6 to J8c4.0			Capt G.F. WOLFE in the outpost line. Sector WESTHOEK RIDGE J.1.d.3.6 to J8 C.4.0 (Ref HOOGE 1/10,000) Sections 1 & 2 & transport moved forward to transport lines at H 28. C 05.05 (Sheet 28 NW)	
J.7.a.5.5.	5/9/17		Four more guns were brought up & relieved 4 guns of the 195th Coy at ZIEL HOUSE to be in support & to carry out a programme of harassing fire in conjunction with the artillery & other M.Gs of the Division.	
	6/9/17		Intersection relief. 2/Lts WOODRUFF & STEADMAN in front line with 4 guns each. 2/Lt RHODES to ZIEL HOUSE. Great artillery activity from 7.30 pm onwards. S.O.S sent up on our front & four guns ZIEL HOUSE fire 1000 rds each before quiet is restored.	
	7/9/17		Day & night comparatively quiet. Harassing fire carried out as per programme. Complaint received from C.O. 2/RIR that a man had been killed in his	

D. D. & L., London, E.C. (A7883) Wt W809/M1672 350,000 4/17 Sch. 52a Forms/C/2118/14

Instructions regarding War Diaries and Intelligence Summaries are contained in F. S. Regs., Part II. and the Staff Manual respectively. Title pages will be prepared in manuscript.

WAR DIARY
or
INTELLIGENCE SUMMARY.
(Erase heading not required.)

Army Form C. 2118.

Place	Date	Hour	Summary of Events and Information	Remarks and references to Appendices
(Contd.)	7.9.17		support line by our MG's. Capts WOLFF + ASHCROFT go to see O.C. 2/R.I.R. + convince him that it was not their guns. Man killed when guns were not firing. C.O. withdraws accusation.	
	8.9.17		All guns relieved by 141st Coy. Relief complete by 12.15 am night of 8th/9th.	
G. 23. b			Taken by bus to DOMINION CAMP, whither 1+2 Sections had proceeded.	
	9.9.17		Cleaning up + Baths. 2/Lt O.W. WALDRON awarded M.C. Sergts RONALD + LAMBOURNE awarded D.C.M.	
	10.9.17		Coy. parade + drill. C of E special Church Parade. 2/Lt O.W. WALDRON awarded M.C.	
	11.9.17		Company less Transport moved by bus to CAESTRE/EECKE area. Transport trek.	
	12.9.17		Company move by route march to HOULERON.	
	13.9.17		— " — " — AUCHEL	
	14.9.17		Intensive training commenced. As per Training Programme attached	
	15.9.17		Training continued. Afternoon holiday.	
	16.9.17		Church Parades.	
	17.9.17		Training continued	
	18/9/17		Training continued	
	19/9/17		Training continued	

D. D. & L., London, E.C.
(A7883) Wt W809/M1672 350,000 4/17 Sch. 52a Forms/C/2118/14

Instructions regarding War Diaries and Intelligence Summaries are contained in F. S. Regs., Part II. and the Staff Manual respectively. Title pages will be prepared in manuscript.

WAR DIARY
or
INTELLIGENCE SUMMARY.
(*Erase heading not required.*)

Army Form C. 2118.

Place	Date	Hour	Summary of Events and Information	Remarks and references to Appendices
AUCHEL	20/9/17		Training Continued. Company attended a Rifle Grenade Barrage demonstration by Canadian School	
	21/9/17		Training continued	
	22/9/17		Training continued. Afternoon Football & Cricket	
	23/9/17		Test of Company in Gas Drill. Smoke Bombs & then with Gas. under Brigade arrangements.	
	24/9/17		Training continued.	
	25/9/17		Training continued as per second Training Programme attached.	
	26/9/17		Divisional Sports at ALLOUAGNE. This Coy awarded the 1st & two 2nd Prizes	
	27/9/17		Training continued. Company attended parade for presentation of decorations by G.O.C 25th Div.	
	28/9/17		Training continued. 2/Lt Watson M.C. Sergts RONALD & LAMBOURNE (D.C.M.) were decorated. Sergt GREEN, L/Cpl LUKE (M.M.) were decorated	
	29/9/17		Training continued. Capt G.T. WOLFF to 48th Course at M.G. School CAMIERS.	
			CAPT ?. E. FABER M.C. from 47th Course at M.G. School CAMIERS. Resumed Command of Company.	
	30/9/17		Church Parades	

W D Lawson Lieut.
~~Capt.~~
Commanding 74th M. G. Company,
Machine Gun Corps.

D. D. & L., London, E.C.
(A7883) Wt. W809/M1672 350,000 4/17 Sch. 52a. Forms/C/2118/14

Time	[illegible]	Sept 15th Saturday	Sept 16 Sunday	Sept 17 Monday	Sept 18 Tuesday	Sept 19th Wednesday	Sept 20th Thursday	Sept 21st Friday	Sept 22nd Saturday	Sept 23rd Sunday	Sept 24 Monday
[illegible]–9.30	Cleaning Billets	NCO's class under C.S.M. cleaning billets		← Cleaning Billets and NCO's class under C.S.M. →							Cleaning Billets NCO's class under C.S.M.
9.0–9.30	Inspections	Company Parade C.21 & 6.2		← Company Parade C.21 & 6.2 →						Church Parades	Company Parade C.21.6.2
9.30–10.30	"A" Formation of Classes – Mechanism – I.A. – Points B.D.A.	"A" class Points B.D.A. "B" " Gun drill "C" " I.A.		"A" Indirect direct fire "B" Gun drill "C" Points B.D.A.	"A" Map & compass "B" I.A. "C" Gun drill	"A" I.A. "B" Overhead direct fire "C" Mechanism	"A" Map & compass "B" Limber drill "C" Gun drill	"A" Barrage fire "B" Pack mule drill "C" I.A.	"A" I.A. "B" Points B.D.A. "C" I.A.		"A" Map & compass "B" Gun drill "C" Mechanism
10.45–12.0		"A" class Mechanism "B" " Points B.D.A. "C" " Mechanism	HOLIDAY.	"A" class Gun drill "B" " Mechanism "C" " I.A.	"A" Limber drill "B" Points B.D.A. "C" I.A.	A, B, C Judging distance	A Pack mule drill B I.A. C Mechanism	"A" Mechanism "B" Mechanism "C" Limber drill	"A" Mechanism "B" I.A. C. Points B.D.A.	HOLIDAY	"A" I.A. "B" Points B.D.A. "C" Gun drill
11.45–12.30		All Physical training and games		← Physical Training and Games for All →							All Physical training and games
2.0–3.0 pm	Company Sergt Major's Parade	Afternoon Football & Cricket		Company Sergt Major's Parade					Afternoon Football & Cricket		C.S.M.'s Parade
				No 2 Section ←	No 3 Section – Range	No 4 Section – C 15 & 05.05	No 1 Section	No 2 Section →			

No 1 Section

No 3

Programme as above to be carried on behind the butts by those not firing with Gas Drill

Section Officers will arrange for occasional "test" gas alarms and carry out Gun Drill and firing in Box Respirators.

Riding practice will be given to the Transport (times to be arranged later).

Lectures to be given whenever outdoor parades are cancelled owing to the weather.

Range takers class
Scouts class
NCO's map reading and report writing class

TIME	25/9 TUESDAY	26/9 WEDNESDAY	SATURDAY 29/9 ~~Thursday~~	28/9 FRIDAY	THURSDAY 27 ~~Saturday~~	30/9 SUNDAY	1/10 MONDAY	2/10 TUESDAY	3/10 WEDNESDAY	4/10 THURSDAY
7 – 7.30 am	Cleaning Billets and N.C.O's class under C.S.M. C21 & 69	Cleaning up	Cleaning Billets and N.C.O's class under C.S.M. C21 & 69			Church Parades	Cleaning Billets and N.C.O's class under C.S.M. C21 & 69			
9 – 9.30 am	Company Parade C21 & 69	Brigade Parade	Company Parade C21 & 69				Company Parade C21 & 69	Field Days under D.M.C.O. at Deserted Village C21 [illegible] including advancing under own barrage		
9.30 – 10.30	[illegible]	Divisional Horse Show and Sports	Scheme for 2 Sections (C 16 and 17)	Scheme for other 2 sections (C 16 & 17)	Class "A" Map & Compass, "B" I.A., "C" Gun Drill		Class "A" Barrage fire, "B" Points B.D.A., "C" I.A.			
10.45 – 11.45	[illegible]		Remaining Section at disposal of Section officer	Remaining Section [illegible] of Section officer	"A" I.A., "B" Mechanism, "C" I.A.	Practice for interbattalion Competition	Class "A" Barrage fire, "B" Stripping and [illegible], "C" Points B.D.A.			
11.45 – 12.30	[illegible]				All P.T. and Games		All P.T. and Games			
[illegible]	[illegible]		Range [illegible] for men with rifles	C.S.M.'s Parade	Games	Games	C.S.M.'s Parade			
[illegible]	[illegible]	No [illegible]	No 1 Section	No 2 Section	No 3 Section		No 4 Section			

Revolver practice as well as M.G. Firing.
M.G. Firing to be combined with Gun Drill & T.O.E.T. and Gas Drill.
Programme [illegible] carried out [illegible] by [illegible] of firing.

[illegible]

Instructions regarding War Diaries and Intelligence Summaries are contained in F. S. Regs., Part II. and the Staff Manual respectively. Title pages will be prepared in manuscript.

WAR DIARY
or
INTELLIGENCE SUMMARY.
(Erase heading not required.)

Army Form C. 2118.

74 MG Coy
Vol 18

Place	Date	Hour	Summary of Events and Information	Remarks and references to Appendices
AUCHEL	1/10/17		Intensive training continued. Special attention was paid to "BARRAGE DRILL" & preparation for competition for B.G.C. Weather fine.	
	2/10/17		Training as above was continued. CO. & 4 officers went to reconnoitre the sector of LENS.	
	3/10/17		Training continued. Company received word to be ready to move immediately to an unknown sector.	
OBLINGHEM	4/10/17	8.45am	Company marched to new Billets at OBLINGHEM. Lieut Lawson was in command of the march. CO. & 4 officers, & 8 NCO's proceeded to reconnoitre the CAMBRIN SECTOR. All the officers & NCO's who went forward remained the night in the line. Lieut COLLEY joined the company from the 195th M.G. Coy.	
CAMBRIN SECTOR	5/10/17	6.30am	Company marched under C.O. to relieve 99th M.G. Coy in the CAMBRIN SECTOR. Fourteen guns were relieved & were grouped in three batteries viz. "A" battery 4 guns – right Sector under Lt Woodruff. "B" Battery 5 guns – left Sector under Lieut Rossiter MC. "C" Battery 5 guns – MAISON ROUGE under 2/Lt Weldrick. Relief was reported complete at 3.15pm. Company H.Q. at ANNEQUIN. CO visited all gun positions. Weather fine	
ANNEQUIN Sheet 36B. F23d.95.95.				

D. D. & L., London, E.C. (A7883) Wt W809/M1672 350,000 4/17 Sch. 52a Forms/C/2118/14

Instructions regarding War Diaries and Intelligence Summaries are contained in F. S. Regs., Part II. and the Staff Manual respectively. Title pages will be prepared in manuscript.

WAR DIARY
or
INTELLIGENCE SUMMARY.
(Erase heading not required.)

Army Form C. 2118.

Place	Date	Hour	Summary of Events and Information	Remarks and references to Appendices
CAMBRIN SECTOR	6/10/17		We found the line abnormally quiet - trenches good - Splendid dug-outs for officers & men. Short resumé of gun positions will be added at the end of the month. "C" Battery at MAISON ROUGE (A26c.48.40 Sheet 36 NW) had a tripod knocked out - no casualties. Previous company's policy of harassing fire by night maintained. Weather very wet.	
	7/10/17		7/10/17 Weather continued to be very wet. Men in billets occupied in improving same. From 10pm to 10.45pm 9 of our guns supported a raid by 46th Division on our right, by putting up a barrage on PARSEVAL ALLEY (G5. c&d Sheet 36c NW. LOOS) Weather cleared. Lt Col Ashworth LAA course	
	8/10/17		At 1am clocks put back one hour - winter time - working party provided for RE's for new emplacement in MUNSTER TUNNEL. Line continues to be very quiet.	
	9/10/17		9/10/17 EA. dropped 3 bombs in F23 d - (Sheet 36B) 3 blinds. Nothing of note in the line. Brigadier General inspected the transport & found everything either "Very Good" or "Excellent". Inter-battery relief.	
	10/10/17		Rain, quiet, cold.	
	11/10/17		Still quiet. 12/10/17 Brigadier General starting at 8.30am visited all gun teams, both batt. H.Q. reconnoitred several new positions leaving line again at 2.30pm. A very strenuous morning.	

D. D. & L., London, E.C. (A7885) Wt W5695/M1672 350,000 4/17 Sch. 52a Forms/C/2118/14

Instructions regarding War Diaries and Intelligence Summaries are contained in F. S. Regs., Part II. and the Staff Manual respectively. Title pages will be prepared in manuscript.

WAR DIARY
or
INTELLIGENCE SUMMARY.
(*Erase heading not required.*)

Army Form C. 2118.

Place	Date	Hour	Summary of Events and Information	Remarks and references to Appendices
CAMBRIN SECTOR	12/10/17		During the past days the Brigadier General expressed to various battalion commanders his approval of the alertness & smartness of the men of this company in the line. Showery	
	13/10/17		& very windy. 13/10/17. Another early morning reconnoitring of the line with the D.M.G.O. Showery, windy (climatically) - line still abnormally quiet. Sgt Critchley this day, to the loss of the company, left it, to become CSM of 145th M.G. Coy.	
	14/10/17		14/10/17 Sunday. Church parades Nonconformist 10.15 am C of E 11.45 am in School at ANNEQUIN. Another reconnaisance of the line. Rum issued daily now. Line still quiet.	
	15/10/17		Early morning reconnaisance of the line. New gun positions temporarily decided upon & sent to DMGO. Weather cold otherwise fine. Two men to Rest Camp & one to Cookery Course BETHUNE. 2/Lt Rhodes. TO. attached for 5 days to A/110 Battery. R.F.A.	
	16/10/17		16/10/17 Weather ~~fine & cold~~ & quietness continue	
	17/10/17		"fine". Usual routine in the line. Harassing fire directed on tracks & C.T.S. rounds fired 11,050. Weather fine but cold.	
	18/10/17		An enemy relief in the sector opposite expected this evening. We fired throughout the night on the tracks & roads enumerated below A29a15.80 & A29a45.40.	

D. D. & L., London, E.C.
(A7883) Wt W809/M1672 350,000 4/17 Sch. 52a Forms/C/2118/14

Instructions regarding War Diaries and Intelligence Summaries are contained in F. S. Regs., Part II. and the Staff Manual respectively. Title pages will be prepared in manuscript.

WAR DIARY
or
INTELLIGENCE SUMMARY.
(Erase heading not required.)

Army Form C. 2118.

Place	Date	Hour	Summary of Events and Information	Remarks and references to Appendices
CAMBRIN SECTOR.	18/10/17		A 29 a 15.00 to A 29 a 50.46 – A 29 a 80.20 to A 29 b 20.70 – A 23 c. 10.40 A 28 b 15.98 to A 28 b 35.85 – A 28 b 12.71 – A 28 b 96.82. A 29 a 50.40 – A 29 a 92.65 The total number of rounds expended, to some purpose, 23,000.	
	19/10/17.		Usual trench routine carried out. Harassing fire directed on chosen targets to the extent of 7400 rounds. Weather fine & cold.	
	20/10/17.		Usual line work. Harassing fire caused expenditure of 9000 rounds.	
	21/10/17.		Sunday. Church parades at ANNEQUIN C. of E. 11.45 am. R.C 10.45 am Nonconformist 10.45 am. This day is the anniversary of the Brigade's successful attack on REGINA TRENCH. The B.G.C. being mightily pleased at the memory gave all the men who took part in that attack, a treat. Fine, cold.	
	22/10/17.		Weather fine but cold. Usual trench routine & harassing fire – number of rounds fired 9500. A bus load of the men of the company were sent from the line to the "Revels" at BETHUNE.	
	23/10/17		Showery weather, making conditions both in & out of the line very miserable. 9000 rounds fired in harassing fire. 24/10/17. Showery &	
	24/10/17		cold. The new battery position at A 20 b 43 for S.O.S. barrage work was taken over. ([illegible])	

D. D. & L., London, E.C. (A7883) Wt W809/M1672 350,000 4/17 Sch. 52a Forms/C/2118/14

Instructions regarding War Diaries and Intelligence Summaries are contained in F. S. Regs., Part II. and the Staff Manual respectively. Title pages will be prepared in manuscript.

WAR DIARY
or
INTELLIGENCE SUMMARY.
(*Erase heading not required.*)

Army Form C. 2118.

Place	Date	Hour	Summary of Events and Information	Remarks and references to Appendices
CAMBRIN SECTOR	24/10/17		over by Lieut ROSSITER MC with 8 guns. Work was commenced on the preparation of the emplacements. The positions at MAISON ROUGE were evacuated for the above purpose. The D.M.G.O visited the battery with the C.O. Weather wretched ~~gale blowing~~.	
	25/10/17		The weather today is wretched - a gale is blowing & heavy rain falling. The battery did good work by sweeping the enemy front line on the whole of the Bgde front to allow active patrolling to proceed. D.M.G.O & O.C. 106th R.E. at battery to finally arrange the details of the new battery emplacements.	
	26/10/17		Weather very wet. The G.O.C. Division visited the battery this morning with D.M.G.O. Usual harassing fire from Right & Left subsector guns. Rounds fired 5000.	
	27/10/17		C.O. spent the night 27/28 visiting all the guns & returned at 5.30 am. Arrangements with Bn Hqtrs made for S.O.S. purposes. Lines laid from 2/Bn H.Q. to "B" Battery H.Q. for S.O.S. communication. Weather improving. B.G.C. visited transport & made splendid report on same	
	28/10/17		Sunday. Usual church parades. R.C. 11 am. C of E 10 am. Nonconformists 11.45 am at ANNEQUIN. Weather fine.	

D. D. & L., London, E.C.
(A7883) Wt W809/M1672 350,000 4/17 Sch. 52a Forms/C/2118/14

Instructions regarding War Diaries and Intelligence Summaries are contained in F. S. Regs., Part II. and the Staff Manual respectively. Title Pages will be prepared in manuscript.

WAR DIARY
or
INTELLIGENCE SUMMARY
(Erase heading not required.)

Army Form C. 2118.

Place	Date	Hour	Summary of Events and Information	Remarks and references to Appendices
CAMBRIN SECTOR	29/10/17		Weather very fine. C.O. went up the line this morning & again in the afternoon. The second time was with C.O. 7th M.G. Coy, a propos of the coming relief by that unit. Two officers of the United States Reserve were attached to us today for instruction. They were Lieut P VANAMEE & 2/Lt H.S. PENNY. C.O. & Lt Dawson spent the night 29/30th showing the U.S.R. officers the line, & the harassing fire work. Fine but very cold.	
	30/10/17		Fine weather again. Attached officers shown the "B" Battery & the barrages etc. C.O. took them to inspect the Transport.	
	31/10/17		Weather again splendid but very cold. Our U.S. guests visited the battery & A/110 battery R.F.A. with C.O. They left us at 3.30pm to return to CAMIERS after expressing their keen delight & thanks for the time they had spent with the company. Good type of men they were and very keen to learn. Lines laid to left Bn H.Q. from "B" Battery for S.O.S. purposes. Work at battery position progressing finely.	

D. R. Dawson Lieut
Capt.
Commanding 74th M.G. Company,
M[illegible] Gun Corps.

2449 Wt. W14957/M90 750,000 1/16 J.B.C. & A. Forms/C.2118/12.

Instructions regarding War Diaries and Intelligence Summaries are contained in F. S. Regs., Part II. and the Staff Manual respectively. Title Pages will be prepared in manuscript.

WAR DIARY
or
INTELLIGENCE SUMMARY
(Erase heading not required.)

Army Form C. 2118.

1/4 Machine Gun Coy

Vol 19

Place	Date	Hour	Summary of Events and Information	Remarks and references to Appendices
CAMBRIN SECTOR.	1/11/17.		The day spent in removing stores etc + relief of the Coy in the line by the 7th M.G. Coy. Relief was complete by 12.30 am 2/11/17. Nos 1 of 8 teams i.e. right + left subsector guns were left in the line to hand over information respecting the guns + the geography of the sector. The company moved on relief to billets at BEUVRY. F14 a.40.20. Weather fine	
BEUVRY F14.a.40.30 sheet 36b.	2/11/17		Training was commenced as per programme to be appended. 16 men i.e. 8 scouts + the 8 Nos 1 + 2 of number 4 section were sent to the Brigade Instructional Platoon for a general course. Weather fine. Remainder of men cleaned up equipment etc. 3/11/17. Training	
	3/11/17.		continued. Half holiday for men. Word received that surplus officers were to report to M.G.C. Base Depot. Weather fine but cold.	
	4/11/17		Sunday. Church parades Roman Catholics. 9. am BEUVRY CHURCH C. of E. CINEMA HALL BEUVRY at 12 noon. Nonconformists CINEMA HALL 10.15 a.m.	
	5/11/17		Weather continues fine 5/11/17. 2/Lts JEFFREY + MARSHALL proceeded to report at M.G.C. BASE DEPOT. Training was continued as per programme. Weather fine. Lt Lawson attached to A/110 Battery for instruction. 6/11/17 Training continued. Attached men of 2 R.I.R.	
	6/11/17		returned to their units. Attached men of 3rd Worcester Regt to replace them	

2449 Wt. W14957/M90 750,000 1/16 J.B.C. & A. Forms/C.2118/12.

Instructions regarding War Diaries and Intelligence Summaries are contained in F. S. Regs., Part II. and the Staff Manual respectively. Title Pages will be prepared in manuscript.

WAR DIARY
or
INTELLIGENCE SUMMARY
(Erase heading not required.)

Army Form C. 2118.

Place	Date	Hour	Summary of Events and Information	Remarks and references to Appendices
BEUVRY	7/11/17		Training continued. Afternoon games. Weather inclement - cold raining	
	8/11/17		8/11/17 Still raining. Programme of work continued indoors.	
	9/11/17		Training continued - weather improved - games indulged in during afternoon.	
	10/11/17		10/11/17. Preparation made for coming relief of the 7th M.G. Coy in the line. Weather very disagreeable.	
CAMBRIN SECTOR.	11/11/17.		The company relieved the 7th Coy in the CAMBRIN SECTOR. 16 guns & teams were taken in & distributed as follows. "B" Battery A20 B. (Sheet 36c NW.) 8 teams under Lieut ROSSITER M.C. Right Subsector 4 teams under Lieut WOODRUFF. Left Subsector 4 teams under 2/Lt RHODES. Relief was complete by 7.30 pm. Weather uncertain & showery.	
	12/11/17.		Harassing fire indulged in to the extent of 3200 rounds. 12/11/17. Usual routine in the line.	
	13/11/17		Harassing fire continued 8500 rounds fired. Weather fine Two guns helped a battalion in raiding operations & taken to the front line for this purpose. In this enterprise to the great loss of the Company Pte Scratcherd was killed.	
	14/11/17.		14/11/17 Raid was undertaken at 6 am & one of our guns silenced an enemy M.G. which was giving trouble 1000 rounds sufficed to do this. Harassing fire expended 6000 rounds. Capt FABER M.C. proceeded on leave.	

Instructions regarding War Diaries and Intelligence Summaries are contained in F. S. Regs., Part II. and the Staff Manual respectively. Title Pages will be prepared in manuscript.

WAR DIARY
or
INTELLIGENCE SUMMARY
(Erase heading not required.)

Army Form C. 2118.

Place	Date	Hour	Summary of Events and Information	Remarks and references to Appendices
~~[illegible]~~ CAMBRIN SECTOR.	15/11/17		Gun Teams in the line relieved by remainder of the Coy from billets. Lt COLLEY to "B" Battery, 2/Lt WELDRICK to LEFT SECTOR. Lt WOODRUFF remains in RIGHT SECTOR. Weather fine. Capt WOLFF returns from Course at Camiers followed by leave & takes over command from Lt LAWSON. Harassing fire carried out by night as usual.	
	16/11/17		Lt LAWSON relieves Lt WOODRUFF in RIGHT SECTOR. Work on battery position carried on by 74th Coy working party. Harrassing Fire each night	
	17/11/17		Working party as usual from 6.30.am to 4.30 pm. One relief. Harassing Fire Day and Night.	
	18/11/17.		Receive Harassing Fire Programme from D.M.G.O. allotting targets & times of firing to 74th, 75th & 9th Coy. This Coy are allotted the biggest share. Fire is directed in conjunction with the Artillery. No Working Party. Church Parades and men allowed on pass from billets to BETHUNE	

HARASSING FIRE PROGRAMME

	DAY					NIGHT				
18th	2 targets	2 guns	1250 rds per gun.	= 2500		2 targets	8 guns	1250 rds per gun	=	10,000
19	2 "	2 "	1250 "	2500		2 "	8 "	1250 "	=	10,000
20	1 "	2 "	1250 "	2500		2 "	6 "	1250 "	=	7500
21	1 "	2 "	1250 "	2500		2 "	7 "	1250 "	=	8750
22	1 "	2 "	1250 "	2500		2 "	7 "	1250 "	=	8750
23	2 "	2 "	1250 "	2500		3 "	7 "	1250 "	=	8750
24	2 "	2 "	1250 "	2500		2 "	8 "	1250 "	=	10000
25	1 "	2 "	1250 "	2500		2 "	8 "	1250 "	=	10000
26	2 "	2 "	1250 "	2500		4 "	8 "	1250 "	=	10000
27	1 "	2 "	1250 "	2500		2 "	8 "	1250 "	=	10000
28	1 "	2 "	1250 "	2500		2 "	6 "	1250 "	=	7500
29	2 "	2 "	1250 "	2500		2 "	7 "	1250 "	=	8750
30	1 "	2 "	1250 "	2500		2 "	8 "	2000 "		16000
				32,500						126000

Total for 13 days = 158,500 rds.

2449 Wt. W14957/M90 750,000 1/16 J.B.C. & A. Forms/C.2118/12.

Instructions regarding War Diaries and Intelligence Summaries are contained in F. S. Regs., Part II. and the Staff Manual respectively. Title Pages will be prepared in manuscript.

WAR DIARY
or
INTELLIGENCE SUMMARY
(Erase heading not required.)

Army Form C. 2118.

Place	Date	Hour	Summary of Events and Information	Remarks and references to Appendices
CAMBRIN SECTOR	19/11/17		Work and H.F. Prog continued. Weather good.	
	20/11/17		Gun teams relieved from billets. Working party only from 6.30 am to 11 am. Officers in line as before.	
	21st + 22nd		Usual Routine. Good work done by Working Parties and Salvage Parties. Night of 22nd two guns placed in front line to keep enemy from repairing his wire. Col FINCH D.S.O. asked for these.	
	23/11/17 24/11/17		Usual Routine. 23rd Sgt White leaves for England to join a Cadet Battalion.	
	25/11/17		Church Parades and no Working Parties. Men in billets allowed passes to BETHUNE	
	26/11/17		All preparations made to support the Infantry in a raid, if called upon to do so. Biggest + most difficult tasks allotted this Coy. Barrage arranged to enfilade within 100x of our objective. 100,000 rds S.A.A got up to positions. M.G's not called for.	
	27/11/17		Gun teams relieved from billets. No working party. Officers in line as before. 2Lt WALDRON. MC returns from leave.	
	28/11/17		Usual Routine - Battery nearly completed.	
	29/11/17		Eight emplacements completed and guns put in. Artillery active.	
	30/11/17		Severe bombardment by Minenwerfer of Old Boots + Reserve trench during afternoon + evening. In the evening battery fire 12,500 rounds at the request of 3rd Worcestershires. Preparations made for relief.	

G Wolff Capt.
Commanding 74th M. G. Company,
Machine Gun Corps.

2449 Wt. W14957/M90 750,000 1/16 J.B.C. & A. Forms/C.2118/12.

Instructions regarding War Diaries and Intelligence Summaries are contained in F. S. Regs., Part II. and the Staff Manual respectively. Title pages will be prepared in manuscript.

WAR DIARY
or
INTELLIGENCE SUMMARY.
(Erase heading not required.)

74th M. G. Coy.

Army Form C. 2118.

Vol 20

Place	Date	Hour	Summary of Events and Information	Remarks and references to Appendices
Cambrin	1/12/17		Weather fine. Relieving Coy Commanders visit H.Q. Raid expected and MG preparations made to meet it. O.C. Coy visits both Batt H.Q in line + leaves one MG Liaison Officer in each. Night quite quiet.	
–"–	2/12/17		Coy relieved by 138th Coy in the line and the 178th Coy at the Battery.	
Beuvry			Relief without a hitch and complete by noon. Billets at BEUVRY.	
LABEUVRIERE	3/12/17		Route march to new billets in LABEUVRIERE. All superfluous stores + kits dumped. Brigade warned to entrain for the SOMME.	
–"–	4/12/17		Entrainment effected without a hitch by noon. Journey slow and very cold. Detrain at ACHIET-le-GRAND about 7 pm + march to billets in ACHIET-le-PETIT. Very cold.	
ACHIET-le-PETIT	5/12/17		Very cold. Day spent preparing for action and a move the next day at 9.30 am.	
–"–	6/12/17		Warned at 3 am to be ready to move at 5 am. Start postponed four hours at 4.30 am.	
BEUGNATRE			March to BEUGNATRE. Billets in a camp.	
–"–	7/12/17		Capt Wolff + the D.M.G.O's 3rd and 25th Divs reconnoitre the line and site 16 new positions for the Coy guns. Line at present held with 7 guns.	

T2134. Wt. W708–776. 500000. 4/15. Sir J. C. & S.

Instructions regarding War Diaries and Intelligence Summaries are contained in F. S. Regs., Part II. and the Staff Manual respectively. Title pages will be prepared in manuscript.

WAR DIARY
or
INTELLIGENCE SUMMARY.
(*Erase heading not required.*)

Army Form C. 2118.

Place	Date	Hour	Summary of Events and Information	Remarks and references to Appendices
BEUGNATRE (contd)	7/12/17		Capt WOLFF returns to camp 6.30 pm. Coy march off at 8 pm and meet guides at VAUX at 9 pm. Relief complete at 2.20 am 8-12-17. Night very dark, roads heavy. All other relieving units except the M.G. Coy are strafed by the B.G.C. for a bad relief.	
MOEUVRES 1/20,000. C.24. D.19. 25+26.	8/12/17		Reconnaissance of line by Acting C.O + Section Officers. New positions started and two battery positions of 4 guns commenced. Sector very quiet + most interesting for M.G.s. Capt FABER. M.C. rejoins Coy from	
—"—			leave + resumes command. Officers in line Lts LAWSON, COLLEY, WOODRUFF, ROSSITER M.C.	
—"—	9/12/17		C.O + 2nd i/c visit lines + decide on final positions of guns. Work carried on every night. Guns defensive, so do not fire. Weather very cold	
—"—	10/12/17		Lt COLLEY, WOODRUFF, LAWSON, relieved by 2/Lts WALDRON, M.C., RHODES, WELDRICK.	
—"—	11/12/17		Work carried on by night. Weather cold.	
—"—	12/12/17		Lt LAWSON relieves Lt ROSSITER, M.C.	
—"—	13/12/17 14/12/17		Work carried on.	
—"—	15/12/17		Lts WOODRUFF, ROSSITER, COLLEY relieve 2/Lts RHODES, WELDRICK, WALDRON M.C. By this time two batteries of four guns with overhead cover + shelters have been	

Instructions regarding War Diaries and Intelligence Summaries are contained in F. S. Regs., Part II. and the Staff Manual respectively. Title pages will be prepared in manuscript.

WAR DIARY
or
INTELLIGENCE SUMMARY.
(Erase heading not required.)

Army Form C. 2118.

Place	Date	Hour	Summary of Events and Information	Remarks and references to Appendices
MOEUVRES 1/20,000 C.24. D.19. 25+26.	15/12/17		made, also seven new secret battle emplacements with overhead cover + shelters + latrines. The whole carefully camouflaged any day.	
—"—	16/12/17		Weather very cold. Improvements on position carried on.	
—"—	17/12/17		The Brgr. General and Capt. Faber M.C. visited all gun positions. Lt. COLLEY took over gun position at C 24 b 83.35 previously held by the 9th Coy. M.G.C.	
	18/12/17		2Lt. Rhodes and 2Lt. Wellrick relieved Lt. Woodruff and Lt. Lawson. Lt. Woodruff and Lt. Mackrell proceeded on leave.	
	19.12.17		Capt. Ashcroft (195th Coy. M.G.C.) and Capt. Faber M.C. visited the gun positions. Lt. Lawson proceeded on leave. 2Lt. Rees joined 2Lt. Rhodes in the line.	
	20/12/17		O/Room moved to new quarters. 'A' Battery, 'B' Battery and 1 gun of the LEFT SECTOR assisted the Infantry, who had suffered severely with hostile machine Guns previous night, Harassing Fire was carried out on the following targets which was sufficient to quieten the enemy:- 1 gun - Target D14 c 65.85 To D14 a 40.30. Rounds fired 500. A Battery - 3 guns - 2 Targets - " " 2750. 'B' Battery - ~~4~~ 3 guns - 3 Targets - " " 3000.	

Instructions regarding War Diaries and Intelligence Summaries are contained in F. S. Regs., Part II. and the Staff Manual respectively. Title pages will be prepared in manuscript.

WAR DIARY
or
INTELLIGENCE SUMMARY.
(Erase heading not required.)

Army Form C. 2118.

Place	Date	Hour	Summary of Events and Information	Remarks and references to Appendices
MOEUVRES 1/20000 C 3rd D 19. 25. 26.	21/12/17		Gun positions improved. weather very cold.	
— " —	22/12/17		Work carried on as usual. Preparations for Company relief.	
— " —	23/12/17		2 new positions were added to "A" Battery now making 6 positions in all. Positions were marked out and work on same commenced.	
			2 new Battery Positions were cited for "B" Battery at D25a 10.50 and C30b 80.65. which were marked out & work commenced on same.	
Sheet 57c 1/40000. H10a 90.40	24/12/17		Company relieved by the 195th Coy. M.G.C. relief complete by 6.30 a.m. Company moved to Camp No 28. H10a 90.40 (Sheet 57c N.W. 1/40000), less Transport. Men proceeded to the Baths and had a general clean up. C.O. taken ill.	
— " —	25/12/17		Xmas Festivities. Xmas Day.	
— " —	26/12/17		Xmas Day celebrations in Camp No 28. Dinner given to men followed by a Concert.	
— " —	27.12.17		Company Training commences. Capt. Faber M.C. takes up position of acting D.M.G.O. and proceeds to Divisional Head Quarters. Capt. Wolff takes over command of Company.	
— " —	28/12/17		Company Training in the morning. Inter-Section Football matches were played in the afternoon.	

T2134. Wt. W708–776. 500000. 4/15. Sir J. C. & S.

Instructions regarding War Diaries and Intelligence Summaries are contained in F. S. Regs., Part II. and the Staff Manual respectively. Title pages will be prepared in manuscript.

WAR DIARY
or
INTELLIGENCE SUMMARY.
(Erase heading not required.)

Army Form C. 2118.

Place	Date	Hour	Summary of Events and Information	Remarks and references to Appendices
Sheet 57C 1/40000 H10a. 90.40	29.12.17		Company Training in the morning. Inter-Section Football matches were played in the afternoon. Lt Rossiter M.C. proceeded to the 3rd. Army School on a course.	
	30.12.17		Xmas Church Parade. Leave camp to relieve 193rd Coy in the line at 2 pm. Limbers packed at Transport. Relief complete by 5.45 pm	
	31.12.17		Day quiet and cold. Capt Fetu M.C. acting D.M.G.O. goes to Hospital.	

G. Wolff Capt.
Commanding 74th M. G. Company
Machine Gun Corps.

T2134. Wt. W708–776. 500000. 4/15. Sir J. C. & S.

COPY No. 9....   SECRET.

RELIEF ORDERS No. 118

1. SMH will relieve MUF in the line, on the afternoon of the 20th inst.

2. 3 limbers & the Officers mess cart will be at Company H.Q. tomorrow at 1-30 pm.
They will be packed as follows:-
1 Limber for blankets and Canteen Stores - blankets to be rolled in bundles of 10, tied and labelled.
1 Limber for Officers valises
H.Q. Limber for Cooks utensils and O/Room boxes.
Mess Cart for Officers mess things.
These vehicles will leave for transport lines at 2 pm from where they will be met by Sections and repacked as follows:-
No 1, 2 & 3 SECTIONS - each 1 limber - containing Guns and equipment for the line. Packs and 1 blanket per man in bundles of 10 and 5 petrol tins of water per Section.
No 4 SECTION. 1 limber - containing packs and blankets as above and Canteen Stores and 6 petrol tins of water (one for Cpl BALLARD).

3. Belt boxes handed over by MUF on last relief will be removed and placed in harness room ready for collection by MUF.

3. Sections will go to positions previously held by them i.e. -
No 1 SECTION under 2/Lt WELDRICK to B BATTERY
No 2 SECTION under 2/Lt RHODES to the RIGHT SECTOR
No 3 SECTION under 2/Lt WALDRON. M.C. assisted by 2/Lt REES to A. BATTERY
No 4 SECTION under Lt COLLEY to the LEFT SECTOR.

4. The four limbers will leave in time to reach SECTION HQ's at 5 pm where they will be met by teams and unpacked immediately.
Section officers will arrange that nothing in the limbers after being unpacked at SECTION HQ
The Transport Sergeant, and 1 Corporal per limber will accompany these vehicles.
The H.Q limber will be repacked to contain C.O's valise. Orderly room boxes and any necessary HQ Stores, and 8 petrol tins of water.
Mess cart will take the necessary stores up the line.
These 2 vehicles will leave in time to reach HQ at 4.30 pm.

5. Sections will march off in time to reach SECTION HQ at 4.45 pm.
H.Q will be marched up by the C.S.M. arriving at 4.15 pm.

6. CPL LIGGETT will arrange to hand over three phones to MUF and take over three phones in the line from MUF.

7. The C.O's horse and Groom to be at Coy H.Q at 2.30 pm.
Section officers will make their own arrangements re their horses.

8. Relief to be complete by 6.30 pm and to be reported by phone to Bn HQ by the code phrase "BMO 30 received"

9. Arrangements must be made by Section Officers that men change their socks + rub their feet with Whale Oil before going on Sentry. Whale Oil will be drawn at C.Q.M.S. Stores while the limbers are being repacked.

10. Reports and returns as during the last tour.

11. The sugar rations will be distributed by the cooks before leaving this Camp.

12. Particular care must be taken that the whole Camp is left scrupulously clean.
The C.S.M will detail men to stop behind for this purpose.

13. The CQMS will hand over to MUF after SMH have left and obtain certificate in writing that everything is clean.

14. ACKNOWLEDGE.

No 1–6 COPIES TO OFFICERS SMH.
" 7 COPY MUF
" 8 " OFFICE
" 9+10 COPIES TO WAR DIARY.

R.A. Colley Lt
O.C. SMH.
DEC. 29TH. 1917.

Instructions regarding War Diaries and Intelligence Summaries are contained in F. S. Regs., Part II. and the Staff Manual respectively. Title pages will be prepared in manuscript.

WAR DIARY
or
INTELLIGENCE SUMMARY.
(Erase heading not required.)

74 M G Coy

Army Form C. 2118.

JANUARY 1918 Vol 21

Place	Date	Hour	Summary of Events and Information	Remarks and references to Appendices
MOEUVRES 1/20.000 PRONVILLE SECTOR	1/1/18		Relief of 195th M.G. Coy carried out without a hitch. The guns in the line were commanded by 2/Lt WELDRICK (No 1 Section), 2/Lt RHODES (No 2 Section) 2/Lt WALDRON (No 3 Sec). Lieut COLLEY (No 4 Sec). Sector very quiet. Weather cold	
	2/1/18		Usual routine in line – great care had to be exercised to keep the guns from becoming frozen up. Weather cold	
	3/1/18.		Weather still cold. Enemy paid rather more attention to back areas with artillery & machine guns causing 1 casualty in our company.	
	4/1/18		Usual routine – weather exceedingly cold. Lts WOODRUFF & MACKRELL returned from leave.	
SHEET 57 C 1/20.000 H.10.a.90.40.	5/1/18.		Company relieved by 195th Coy & proceeded to No 28 Camp. Relief complete by 6.30 pm. Lt LAWSON returned from leave.	See Relief Orders No 117 attd.
	6/1/18.		Gun equipment cleaned & limbers packed in readiness to take up emergency positions in line as quickly as possible. Training as per programme attached commenced	
	7/1/18		Training continued – work on bomb proof parapets round huts commenced. Capt FABER MC resumes work as A/D.M.G.O.	
	8/1/18		Training continued – weather warmer – slight thaw & frost again	
	9/1/18		Training continued. 2/Lt RHODES & 24 men worked all night 9/10 on new positions at D2 Battery. Weather extremely inclement. Thaw commences.	

A5834 Wt. W4973 M687 750,000 8/16 D. D. & L. Ltd. Forms/C.2118/13.

Instructions regarding War Diaries and Intelligence Summaries are contained in F. S. Regs., Part II. and the Staff Manual respectively. Title pages will be prepared in manuscript.

WAR DIARY
or
INTELLIGENCE SUMMARY.
(Erase heading not required.)

Army Form C. 2118.

Place	Date	Hour	Summary of Events and Information	Remarks and references to Appendices
Sheet 57c H.10 a. 90·40	10/1/18		Training continued during these days but work greatly hampered by the thaw and rain. Football played one afternoon only	
Camp 28.	11/1/18		Training limited to Coy parades, indoor instruction and one hours squad + arms drill	
	12/1/18			
MOEUVRES 1/20,000 PRONVILLE SECTOR.	13/1/18		Morning inspection. Camp 28 vacated at 2 pm + Company proceeds to craft lanes to pack limbers. 3.15 pm Sections move off to relieve 195th Coy in the line PRONVILLE SECTOR. No 4 Section in B2 battery, No 1 in B Battery, No 3 in A Battery, No 2 in valley positions ADAM, APPLE, ALLELUIA, AMEN. Coy HQ with Brigade as before. Relief complete by 7 pm. Freezing again.	See Relief Orders No 127 attd.
	14/1/18		Day cold + quiet. Work continued on all positions.	
	15/1/18		Thaw sets in + weather very wet.	
	16/1/18		Trenches and emplacements falling in badly. Great discomfort for Sections 1+3 in 34 + 35 posts as Dug Outs falling in + being flooded. Pumps provided + after hard work dug outs made habitable. 2/Lt F.O. RHODES proceeds on leave.	
	17/1/18		Work continues on trenches, dug-outs + emplacements. B2 battery vacated + Nos 5 6 7 + 8 positions occupied	
	18/1/18		Weather slightly better. Coy H.Q. moved forward to Deep Dug Out J 2 b. 20·72.	
	19/1/18		16 O.R. proceed on leave, all of them having been one year without it	
	20/1/18		Work carried on as usual. Weather fine. H.Q shelled from 10am to 4 pm. Night quiet	
	21/1/18		Shelters improved + new ones built. Emplacements improved. H.Q shelled from 7am	
	22/1/18		Weather good. Coy. Hdqrs moved to deep dug out C.24 d 65·70.	
	23/1/18		Work at B Battery position finished by No 1 Section	
	24/1/18		5th position at B Battery completed ready for use in case of emergency. 2/Lt Weldrick [?] returned from leave U.K.	

A5834 Wt. W4973 M687 750,000 8/16 D. D. & L. Ltd. Forms/C.2118/13.

Instructions regarding War Diaries and Intelligence Summaries are contained in F. S. Regs., Part II. and the Staff Manual respectively. Title pages will be prepared in manuscript.

WAR DIARY
or
INTELLIGENCE SUMMARY.
(Erase heading not required.)

Army Form C. 2118.

Place	Date	Hour	Summary of Events and Information	Remarks and references to Appendices
	25/1/18		6th Position at 'B' Battery completed. Weather still good. 2/Lt Wildrick joined no 1 section in the line. Sector quiet.	
	26/1/18		Company relieved by sections of the 7th and 75th companies. Relief completed without any event of importance. Company billeted at no 28 camp.	
	27/1/18		Church Parades for Roman C's and Pres were held in the morning, remainder of company packed limbers in accordance with Defence Scheme. Evening a C of E was held in camp.	
	28/1/18		Fighting limbers were brought from Transport lines to no 28 camp. Arrangements made whereby officers (one in turn) had permission to spend a day in Amiens. Hostile planes bombed billets and transport lines and dumps in neighbourhood of 28 camp for about 3 hours.	
	29/1/18		Capt Wolff proceeded to Warloy to attend an RFC course. Lt Pawson took over command of company during former's absence. Vicinity of 28 camp again bombed by hostile planes. 7 bombs fell within 100 yds of camp. Trenches were dug away from camp for protection for men in case of further raids.	
	30/1/18		Weather frosty. Training continued, consisting of squad, arms, and gun drill. Hostile planes again visited area during the night but did not remain long.	
	31/1/18		Lt Woodruff + 2/Lt Rees reconnoitred line previous to company taking over positions from 198th Coy. Training continued. Weather misty and frosty	

W. H. Pawson Capt.
Commanding 74th M. G. Company,
Machine Gun Corps.

A5834 Wt. W4973/M687 750,000 8/16 D. D. & L. Ltd. Forms/C.2118/13.

COPY No. 10. SECRET.

RELIEF ORDERS. No 119.

1. SMH. will be relieved by MUF on the evening of the 5th inst at dusk, as follows:-
No 3 & 1 SECTIONS by MUF 2 & 4 Sections under 2/Lt HIND & Lt. YOUNG with No 2 on the right.
No 2. SECTION by MUF No 3 Section under 2/Lt WILKINS.
No 4 SECTION by MUF No 1 Section under Lt BRUTTON

2. SMH. will hand over all gear less guns, spare barrels, spare parts boxes, condenser tubes & bags, clinometers & petrol tins, obtaining receipts in duplicate, one of which will be handed to Ofroom by 10 am 6th inst, together with a certificate, that everything has been handed over in clean & good condition.
Maps QUEANT & VAULX-VRAUCOURT will not be handed over.
TELEPHONES. - CPL. LIGGETT will hand over the three phones taken over by him, and take over SMH three phones at No 28 Camp.
No 2. Section will be responsible for bringing out the phone at LEECH AVENUE.

3. MUF limbers will carry out SMH guns, packs, blankets etc.

Blankets will be rolled in bundles of 10 and tied.
Limbers will proceed direct to No 28 Camp with the exception of the limber carrying No 1. Sections guns, which will go to SMH Transport lines to be unloaded.
No 1. Section will be billeted at Transport lines.

4. The C.Q.M.S. will take over No 28 Camp at 2.45 pm 5th inst. He will take the Company books with him.
He will arrange to issue to Sections H.Q their second blanket.
He will arrange for water cart to visit camp & that hot drinks are ready for the Company at 8 pm.

5. CANTEEN. L/Cpl BALLARD will remain in the line until the evening of the 6th when he will come down with the empty ration limbers of MUF.
Tomorrow evening his rations will come up with MUF No 1 Section rations.

6. ANTI-AIRCRAFT. O.C. No 2 Section will detail 1. NCO and 6 reliable gunners to report at Company HQ at 3 pm 5th inst.

for duty with Brigade Anti-Aircraft guns, they will remain with Brigade H.Q.

Their rations will be sent up daily with Brigade H.Q. rations.

7. One MGF limber & Officers mess cart will ~~will~~ bring in MGF HQ and will take out SMH. H.Q.

Capt Wolff's horse will be at VAUX X ROADS at 6.15pm 5/12/17.

8. MGF will hand over to CQMS SMH filled belt boxes to the number of 18 per gun as near as is possible, and 16 tripods, when he takes over No 28 Camp on 5th inst.

9. ACKNOWLEDGE

COPIES No 1 – 6 OFFICERS. SMH
COPY No 7 MGF
No 8 OFFICE
COPIES No 9 & 10 WAR DIARY
COPY No 11. C.Q.M.S. SMH.

J. Wolff Capt
O.C. SMH.

Dec. 4th. 17.

COPY No. 11 SECRET.

RELIEF ORDERS No 127.

1. SMH will relieve MUF in the line on the afternoon of 13th inst.

2. 4 Limbers and the Officers mess cart will be at Company H.Q. tomorrow at 1.30 pm.
They will be packed as follows:–
1 Limber for blankets (1 per man) to be rolled in bundles of 10 and taken into the line.
1 Limber for blankets (1 per man) to be rolled in bundles of 10 and taken to CQMS Stores.
1 Limber for Officers valises
HQ Limber for books utensils and O'Room Boxes
MESS CART for Officers mess things
These vehicles will leave for Transport Lines at 2 pm prompt where they will be met by Sections and repacked as follows:–
No 1.2.3 & 4 SECTIONS each 1 limber containing – Guns, equipment etc for line. mess packs and 1 blanket per man rolled in bundles of 10. and 5 Petrol tins of water per Section.
L/Cpl. CUMMINGS. will accompany No 3 Section and cook for A & B. BATTERIES, taking with him 4 Dixies.
No 2. SECTION will take 1 dixie into the line.
Canteen boxes will be left at CQMS Stores in charge of L/Cpl. BALLARD and 1 other man. They will come up the line with rations on the evening of the 14th.
Belt boxes handed over by MUF on last relief will be removed and placed in Harness Room ready for collection by them. Also the 14 tripods taken over from MUF.

3. Sections will go to positions as follows:–
No 1 SECTION to "B" BATTERY under Lt. LAWSON
No 2 --- " RIGHT SUB-SECTOR as before under Lt. WOODRUFF.
No 3 --- " "A" BATTERY under Lt. WALDRON. M.C. assisted by 2/Lt. REES.
No 4 --- " "B2" BATTERY under Lt. COLLEY.
4 Guides from MUF will meet No 4 Section at LEFT SECTOR H.Q and lead teams to their new positions.

4. The 4 limbers will leave in time to reach SECTION H.Q's at 5pm where they will be met by teams and unpacked immediately.
Section Officers will arrange that nothing is in the Limbers after being unpacked at Section H.Q.
The Transport Officer and 1 corporal per limber will accompany these vehicles.

The H.Q Limber will be repacked to contain C.O's Valise Orderly Room boxes and any necessary H.Q Stores and 8 Petrol tins of water.
Mess Cart will take the necessary stores up the line.
These 2 vehicles will leave in time to reach Coy H.Q at 4.30pm

5. Sections will march off in time to reach SECTION H.Q at 4.45pm.
H.Q will be marched up by the A/C.S.M. arriving at 4.15pm.

6. CPL. LIGGETT. will arrange to take S.M.H 4 phones into the line.
He will install 3 as previously arranged.

7. The C.O's horse and Groom to be at Coy H.Q at 2.30pm 13/1/18.
Section Officers will make their own arrangements re their horses.

8. Relief to be complete by 5.30pm and to be reported by phone to Company H.Q by the code phrase "BMO 13 received".

9. Arrangements must be made by Section Officers that men change their socks before going on Sentry.
Whale oil & rations will be drawn at C.Q.M.S Stores while Limbers are being repacked.

10. Reports and Runners as during the last tour.

11. Tea & Sugar rations will be distributed by the cooks before leaving this Camp.

12. Particular care must be taken that the whole camp is left scrupulously clean.
2/Lt. RHODES and 7 men proceeding on leave the 15th inst will stay behind and clean the camp.

13. 2/Lt. RHODES will hand over to M.U.F. immediately S.M.H has left the Camp and obtain Certificate in writing that everything is clean.

14. ACKNOWLEDGE.

W. D. Lawson Lieut
HADJT.
S.M.H.
JAN 12 18

No 1 — 8 COPIES TO OFFICERS SMH
" 9 COPY TO M.U.F
" 10 " " OFFICE
" 11-12 COPIES TO WAR DIARY.

[illegible] No. 11

RELIEF ORDERS. No. 128

Ref Map Sheet 57c 1/40,000.

1. SMH will be relieved on the evening of the 26th inst as follows:
   No 1 Section by No 1 Section A.C.H
   No 2 — " — " No 2 — " — A.C.H
   No 3 — " — " No 3 — " — A.C.H
   No 4 — " — " [illegible] Section of V.C.H

2. SMH will hand over all [illegible] guns, [illegible] spare parts boxes, [illegible], clinometers & patrol [illegible] at Gun positions, obtaining receipts in duplicate, one of which [illegible] be handed to Ofroom by 10 am 27th inst, together with a certificate that everything has been handed over in clean and good condition.
   [illegible] QUEANT & VAULX-VRAUCOURT will not be handed over.
   [illegible] care will be taken that all information, calculations and work to be done etc are correctly handed over.
   No 4 Section will hand over "B2" Battery stores and Section HQ to No 4 Section A.C.H.
   They will hand over Nos 5, 6, 7 & 8 Gun positions and stores belonging thereto and the shelter now used as a store, to a Section of V.C.H.
   TELEPHONES will be taken over [illegible] the Company.
   [illegible] will be relieved early on the 26th inst and will report to Coy HQ whence they will [illegible] to No 28 Camp under Cpl Liggett [illegible] telephone [illegible].

3. A.C.H limbers will take out Nos 1, 2, 3 [illegible] [illegible] HQ to No 28 Camp.
   V.C.H limber will take out No 4 Section to No 28 Camp.
   Blankets will be rolled in bundles of 10, tied and labelled.
   At No 28 Camp limbers will be unloaded by their respective Sections.

4. The CQMS will take over No 28 Camp [illegible] 26th inst.
   Ptes WATSON No 3 Section & JEWELL No 1 [illegible] [illegible] at Transport Lines [illegible] [illegible].
   The CQMS will take [illegible] [illegible] [illegible] [illegible] rations to No 28 Camp.
   He will arrange for the water cart to report at No 28 Camp and that [illegible] ready for the [illegible] on arrival about 9 pm.
   He will take over 4 [illegible] [illegible] [illegible] from V.C.H [illegible] [illegible] Room at Transport Lines.

5. The T.O. will arrange for [illegible] [illegible] [illegible] to [illegible] No 28 Camp.

[illegible] [illegible] & [illegible] will remain in the [illegible] until [illegible] [illegible] They will come down with the empty ration [illegible] [illegible]

[illegible] [illegible] [illegible] rations will be brought [illegible] [illegible] Guide of [illegible] Section.

[illegible] [illegible] [illegible] SMG HQ at [illegible]pm [illegible]

Guides [illegible] [illegible] [illegible]:-

[illegible] [illegible] at the Transport Lines at 4pm & take [illegible] [illegible] [illegible] No 1 2 3 & 4 Section HQ and HQ Limbers [illegible]

V.C.H Limbers — will not require a Guide.

One Guide from each Section and 1 from HQ will be at [illegible] [illegible] SMG HQ [illegible] at 5.30pm to guide A.C.H. Sections [illegible] [illegible] [illegible] they will be guided to [illegible] [illegible] [illegible].

One Guide from No 4 Section will be at the same spot at 5pm to meet the Section of V.C.H & Guide them to No 4 Section [illegible] whence they will be guided to No 5 6 7 8 positions.

[illegible] Guides mounted or otherwise will have a written slip [illegible] [illegible] [illegible] he is taking the incoming party also the number of the Company he is expecting to guide in.

[illegible] Sections will leave a "No 1" at each of the following positions No 1 2 3 & 4 [illegible] [illegible] "A" "B" "B2" [illegible] who will remain there until 5.30pm 27th inst.

The C.Q.M.S. will arrange to send up rations for these men [illegible] [illegible] [illegible] [illegible] by A.C.H ration limbers the night of 27th inst. [illegible] Section Officer [illegible] [illegible] [illegible] when handing over.

10. The Transport Officer will arrange to take [illegible] [illegible] A.C.H. [illegible] 12 tripods & 84 filled Belt boxes, dumping them in [illegible] [illegible] Room.

11. Rifles and Revolvers will be inspected [illegible] [illegible] relief.

12. Relief will be reported complete [illegible] HQ by runner or phone by the message "SMG all received".

13. ACKNOWLEDGE.

[illegible] [illegible] [illegible] SMH
" 8 T.O. SMH
" " 9 CQMS SMH
" " 10 OFFICE
" No 11/12 WAR DIARY
" No 13 A.C.H.
" " 14 V.C.H.

[signature] Capt.
O.C. SMH

JAN 25TH. 18.

Army Form C. 2118.

Instructions regarding War Diaries and Intelligence Summaries are contained in F. S. Regs., Part II. and the Staff Manual respectively. Title pages will be prepared in manuscript.

WAR DIARY
or
INTELLIGENCE SUMMARY.
(Erase heading not required.)

Place	Date	Hour	Summary of Events and Information	Remarks and references to Appendices
Ref Map Sheet 57c				
Camp 6 (old No 28) Sheet 57c	1/2/18.		Training and work on bomb protection at Trspt Lines continued. Weather frosty.	
H. 10. c. 8.8.	2/2/18.		Lt LAWSON goes to Left Sub Sector at 6 am to arrange relief of 195th Coy. Capt WOLFF returns from ~~base~~ course at 3rd Squadron R.F.C. Vacate camp 6 at 2 pm + move to Transport Lines. Leave Trspt Lines about 3.15 pm for area C. 16·17 + 23. Relief complete by 8 pm. Night quiet.	Relief Orders attached
C. 16·17 + 23.	3/2/18.		Day quiet. Work done on emplacements. Positions held are Nos 9, 10. 11, 12.13, 14. 15. 16 17, 18.19. F Battery, 2 guns; F2 Battery, 3 guns.	
— " —	4/2/18		Day quiet. Work continued.	
— " —	5/2/18.		Hostile Strafe at 6.30 am along road thro' C. 17. b + d. Remainder of day and night quiet. Work continued. 500 rds Harassing Fire by No 14 gun from WAKEFIELD AVENUE.	
— " —	6/2/18		Day + night quiet. Weather fine work as usual. 1750 rds Harassing Fire by No 14 gun from WAKEFIELD AVENUE. Work as usual.	
— " —	~~7/2/18~~		~~Day quiet, weather damp.~~ Lt LAWSON + Sergt GREEN leave line for Trspt Lines to proceed on III Army Infantry Course. Lt COLLEY rejoins Coy in the line from DIV. Rest Camp.	
— " —	7/2/18.		Weather damp. Day quiet. Some shelling at night, probably due to Infantry relief. War Savings campaign opened.	
— " —	8/2/18		Day quiet. Weather fine. O.C. 16th Coy visits line to arrange relief.	
— " —	9/2/18		Day quiet. Weather fine. Officers of 16th Coy visit line. Also Major D. Drummond D.S.O.	
— " —	10/2/18		Day + night quiet. Work continued.	
— " —	11/2/18		Coy relieved in line by 16th Coy. Relief complete by 7.45 pm. Coy move out to No 5 Camp.	Relief Orders attached
H 10 c.2·5				

A5834 Wt. W4973 M687 750,000 8/16 D. D. & L. Ltd. Forms/C.2118/13.

Instructions regarding War Diaries and Intelligence Summaries are contained in F. S. Regs., Part II. and the Staff Manual respectively. Title pages will be prepared in manuscript.

WAR DIARY
or
INTELLIGENCE SUMMARY.
(Erase heading not required.)

Army Form C. 2118.

Place	Date	Hour	Summary of Events and Information	Remarks and references to Appendices
	12/2/18.		Coy parade. Clean + pack limbers. March off for new billets at 2 pm to ACHIET-le-PETIT. March past D.M.G.O + a/D.M.G.O. Join the other three companies in BUCHANON CAMP.	Orders attached.
G.14.b. 60.75.	13/2/18		Day wet. Work on bomb protection. Afternoon baths.	
	14/2/18		Work on huts continued.	
	15/2/18		ditto Kit inspection + general clean up. Hut inspection. The four MG Coys in camp as a battalion. Major J. D. Deane-Drummond D.S.O, M.C. in command. Capt. L.K. Faber 2nd i/c. New battalion organisation started on the 13th (unofficially).	
	16/2/18		Work on huts completed.	
	17/2/18		Church Parades etc.	
	18/2/18		Training started. Capt Faber M.C. appointed 2nd i/c officially.	
	19/2/18		Training continued.	
	20/2/18		Baths + training.	
	21/2/18		Training continued	
	22/2/18 } 23/2/18 }		— " — 23/2/18. Lieuts COLLEY + WALDRON, M.C. proceed on leave.	
	24/2/18		Battalion Sports + Church Parades.	
	25/2/18 } 26/2/18 }		Training	
	27/2/18		Indirect fire on Range. Capt WOLFF appointed to command 74th Coy.	
	28/2/18		Inspection of Battalion less 7th Coy by IV Corps commander	

[signature] Capt.
Commanding 74th M. G. Company,
Machine Gun Corps.

A5834 Wt. W4973 M687 750,000 8/16 D. D. & L. Ltd. Forms/C.2118/13.

COPY No. 17... **RELIEF ORDERS No. 136.** SECRET.

REF: MAP 57C 1/40,000

I. On the afternoon of the 11th inst. Transport and C.Q.M.S. stores and details will vacate WACKLANDS LINES and proceed to No. 5 camp (H10 c 2.5.) which will be shared with 75th Coy M.G.C.
Riding Horses and grooms will be left at WACKLANDS LINES for the night of the 11th/12th by arrangement with the 16th Coy.
The T.O. will arrange to take over the new billets and hand over the old lines, obtaining the usual receipts and certificates.
Transport will be picketed in field adjoining No. 5 CAMP.
The evening of the 11th the Coy. in the line will be relieved by the 16th Coy.

II Scouts from LT. WOODRUFF, 2ND LTS. RHODES, and WALDRICK will report at Coy. H.Q. at 3pm on the 11th whence they will be taken by two other scouts to York Roads C.25 d 70.70 arriving at 3.45pm to guide the four Sections and H.Q of the 16th Coy. to the York Roads near Coy. H.Q. with the exception of 2ND LT. RHODES scout who will guide the limber and relief for 1 and 2 BATTERIES direct to Section H.Q. where they will be met by five guides.
One guide per gun from Nos. 9 – 19 will be at York Roads C23 b 55.75 at 4.30 pm to guide incoming teams to positions. Each guide will have a slip bearing the No of the gun from which he comes.

III The following will be handed over,

Tripods less Cross Heads,
14 Belt Boxes per gun,
All trench stores, reserve oil and paraffin,
All information, calculations and S.O.S. lines,
All maps other than those of scales 1/250,000, 1/100.000 & 1/40,000.

Reserve Petrol tins will not be handed over.
Receipts and handing over certificates to be sent to O/Room by 11am on the 13th inst.

IV Limbers will report as follows:-
2 limbers for No. 3 Section and 1 team of No: 2 Section to No: 3 Section H.Q. (C 16 b) at 5.45 pm.
1 limber for No: 4 Section's Nos. 12 and 13 guns and part of H.Q to be at York Roads (C 23 b 55.75) at 5.30 pm.
1 limber for No: 2 Section's Nos. 9, 10 & 11 guns to be at York Roads (C 23 b 55.75) at 5.45 pm.
1 limber for No. 1 Section for Nos: 14, 15, 16 & 17 guns to be at York Roads (C 23 b 55.75) at 6 pm.
1 limber for No. 4 Section for Nos 18 and 19 guns and part of H.Q if necessary to be at York Roads (C 23 b 55.75) at 6 pm.
1 limber for H.Q. to be at York Roads (C 23 b 55.75) at 5.15 pm.

V. Signallers will come out with the Sections to which they are attached bringing out their phones.

VI. Relief complete to be reported by phone or runner by the Code Phrase "B.M.O. 11 received"

VII. On relief Sections will proceed to No. 5 Camp. (H.10.c.2.5)

VIII. C.O's horse to be at VAULX at 7 p.m.

IX. Hot drinks will be issued on arrival in Camp, about 8.30 p.m.

X. ACKNOWLEDGE

R.A. Colley Lt. O/C 207th(?)
M.G. Coy.
FEB. 9th 1918.

Copies	Nos.	1 – 7	Officers	M.G. Coy.
Copy	"	8	T.O.	" "
"	"	9	C.S.M.	" "
"	"	10	O.C. 16th M.G. Coy.	
"	"	11	FILE(?)	
Copies	"	12–13	WAR DIARY	

Addition.

A ~~[illegible]~~ man will stay with each gun until "Stand down" on the morning of the 12th when they will march down to No 5 Camp.

Copy No. 11... MOVE ORDERS No 138 SECRET.

Ref. MAP 57^c 1/40,000.

1. The Coy will parade ready to move to its new billets at BUCHANAN CAMP (D." Bn) G 14 b 60.70 ACHIET AREA at 2 pm on the 12TH inst. in column of route on road outside No. 5 Camp. facing S.
2. Officers Valises will be placed at C.Q.M.S. Stores by 12 midday.
3. Blankets will be rolled in bundles of 10, tied, labelled and dumped at C.Q.M.S stores by 9.30 am.
4. The Mess Cart will be at Officers Mess at 1 pm and will be packed at once.
5. The T.O. will arrange how all stores are to be carried.
6. A lorry for this Coy will report to No. 5 Camp at 10 am.
7. Limber Corporals will report their limbers correctly packed to LT COLLEY by 1.30 pm.

ROUTE. SAPIGNIES – BIHUCOURT.

The O/Officer will satisfy himself that the Camp is left clean and render a certificate to O/Room.

R.A. Colley Lt A/ADJT.
11.2.18.

Copies Nos 1-8 Officers 7th M.G. Coy.
Copy " 9 C.S.M.
" " 10 File.
Copies " 11-12 War Diary.

www.ingramcontent.com/pod-product-compliance
Lightning Source LLC
Chambersburg PA
CBHW081552160426
43191CB00011B/1909